BEYOND 2020

LIFE AND BUSINESS LESSONS ON THRIVING AMIDST A PANDEMIC

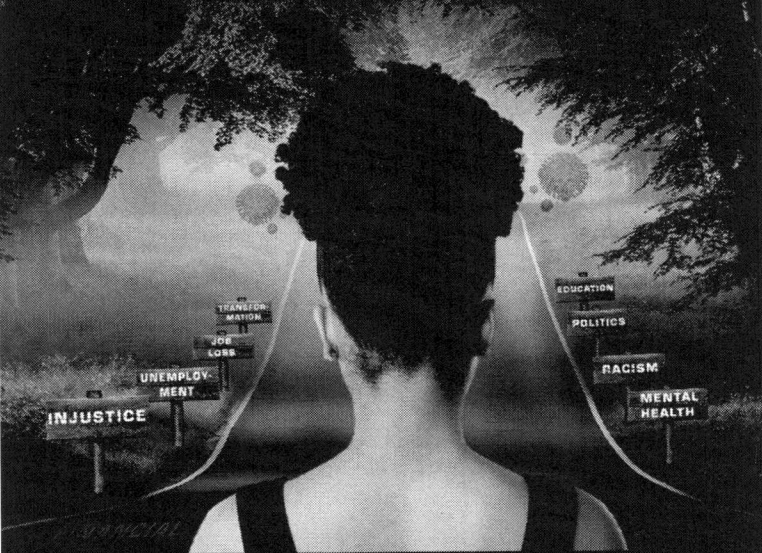

TRANSFOR-
MATION

EDUCATION

JOB
LOSS

POLITICS

UNEMPLOY.
MENT

RACISM

INJUSTICE

MENTAL
HEALTH

COMPILED BY:

Lynn Richardson

FOREWORD BY LANA "MC LYTE" MOORER

TABLE OF CONTENTS

BEYOND 2020

LIFE AND BUSINESS LESSONS ON THRIVING AMIDST A PANDEMIC

TRANSFOR-MATION

JOB LOSS

UNEMPLOY-MENT

INJUSTICE

EDUCATION

POLITICS

RACISM

MENTAL HEALTH

COMPILED BY:

Lynn Richardson

FOREWORD BY LANA "MC LYTE" MOORER

FOREWORD

Lana "MC Lyte" Moorer

Sure, there have been many books published that have compiled short stories from various writers. There have been books that have gathered African American writers which have given an account of their lives and allowed them to share their experiences. This book differs because Dr. Lynn Richardson has hand selected this specific group of women from her New W.E.A.L.T.H. University Author's Collaboration Circle. In 2020, these accomplished and successful women came together and created a circle of trust and accountability. Dr. Lynn has now invited these 14 dynamic women to come forward and share what is on their minds, but most importantly, what is in their hearts.

These beautiful black sisters come from all walks of life and each with a different perspective and story to tell. They speak of love, loss, strength, and courage, all while remaining transparent and candid in opening themselves.

Enjoy the power that lies within the words and between the lines as you thrive Beyond 2020!

INTRODUCTION

Dr. Lynn Richardson

I quit my job, but soon afterwards got the opportunity of my dreams working for a global icon. Next thing you know, the market crashed, and I ended up in foreclosure, bankruptcy, and ironically, full of hope. So, I created W.E.A.L.T.H. Vision 20/20. It was my vision that by the year 2020, I would have a clear view on my path towards helping others become financially free. It was my vision that others would have a clear path, lit with 20/20 vision, to obtain a financial education. That was 2008.

Fast forward.

2020. I have a lot of jobs.

TV Personality.

Life Coach.

Pastor.

Mom.

Wife.

And I'm really tired of traveling. Help me Lord, I pray.

I already know there's more that I can do. But I don't want to do anything at all. I need rest!

But wait . . . I promised God that if He saved me from myself (back in 2006), I would live my life according to His will and not my own.

So, I cried about it. I was tired, remember?

Then I did something about it!

I expanded New W.E.A.L.T.H. University to finally give people around the globe an affordable education. Let's go!!

But wait a minute.

What?

A pandemic??

What in the world is a pandemic?

Quarantine.

Stop!!

But I didn't get to stop. I had to go. I had to operate on autopilot working with technology, marketing, and the mass media to educate people about the very thing I've been saying forever: EVERYBODY NEEDS A HOMEBASED BUSINESS!! Why? Because one stream of income is hazardous to your wealth! Now we're in a recession and it's worse than 2008. You can't just go and look for a job. You can't even go out with your friends to laugh or cry about it.

Stay in the house.

That's what I did.

For a year.

And what I learned is this:

If you can survive 2020, you can thrive anywhere, anytime, and beyond anything.

This time, I'm not in foreclosure. I'm not bankrupt. My children are educated.

I have lived the vision: W.E.A.L.T.H. Vision 20/20; and I'm helping others live it too.

And the best part . . . I still drive a 2005 Mercedes though I can purchase any vehicle I want! Why? Because I don't NEED a new vehicle: I don't even like to drive, and as a result, I don't get behind the wheel more than once a quarter. So I no longer acquire things as status symbols. Living Beyond 2020 means understanding the difference between needs and wants and strategically leveraging our resources so we can build generational wealth. Living Beyond 2020 means getting your emotions in check and making wise decisions pertaining to your money, your time, your energy and your circle. Living Beyond 2020 means living within God's Will, God's Way and in God's time.

How do you do this? The same way I do:

Trust the Lord with all of your heart. Lean not on your own understanding. Acknowledge God in all your ways and He will direct your path.
Proverbs 3: 5-6

Now thrive . . . BEYOND 2020!

ACKNOWLEDEGMENTS

Thank you to all of my students, colleagues, instructors, family and friends.

Thank you to my daughters for quarantining (Cydney in Chicago and Taylor & Kennedy at home in California while awaiting your return to Howard University) and working with me as we build the Richardson Dynasty.

Thank you to the love of my life, Demietrius, for being right by my side each day. Congratulations on your promotion!

Thank you to each and every person who will read this and choose to THRIVE BEYOND 2020.

And last, but certainly not least, thank you to the inaugural AUTHOR'S COLLABORATION CIRCLE. You exhibit greatness!

Go and get EVERYTHING that God has for you!

Lynn Richardson™

ARE YOU READY FOR THE CHANGE?

MICHELLE SENDERSON

"The only constant in life is change" – Heraclitus, Greek philosopher

As a corporate executive in a Fortune 100 Company, I would often ask, "Are you ready for the change?"

A few years ago, the environment was prevalent with outsourcing, automation and robotic elements replacing repetitive tasks performed by humans. Each one of these factors generally led to reduced roles in the workplace. Given the times, I often asked individuals to constantly assess their skillsets to prepare for the unexpected. I also frequently taught success principles on how to remain at the top of one's game. The team often thought that I was preparing them for what to do if they lost their job, but few realized I was providing the blueprint for what to do if they remained. Change is evident.

March 2020, absolutely nothing could have prepared this Piscean for the disruption to come after a girl's night out in New York City in celebration of my birthday. The drive to the restaurant was surrounded by a cloud of tension in the air. Oddly, the streets were eerily quiet even though it was the middle of rush hour. The Maître D' only allowed entry after lavishly spraying our hands with an alcohol mist and scanning our driver licenses. "What!! When did we have to start doing this to enter a fine dining establishment?"

A few days later, a shelter in place order was declared in the United States to stop the spread of the coronavirus, essentially putting LIFE on pause for several months. It was as if God had hit the pause button on the remote and the world froze in time. We had entered a GLOBAL PANDEMIC!

The question then becomes, "What do you do when the script has flipped and the whole world has stopped?" ARE YOU READY FOR THE CHANGE?

I then realized the question I asked so many times of others, I now had to ask myself. To be transparent, I felt far from ready. I began to fret and stress over items I could not control and I struggled with the day to day. Conversations with friends and family proved fruitless as they struggled with the same feelings. This was deep. My mind then quickly went back to a statement made by Bishop T.D. Jakes. He stated, "You need to eat on the level of your vision". No matter the circumstances or obstacles, set your mind on HIGH. Stay hopeful and elevate your mindset.

Even though we are in a global pandemic, use the time to RESET, RENEW and EVOLVE to YOUR GREATER SELF. Be ready in and out of season. Tap into your talents and step into your divine purpose.

The pandemic has leveled the playing field. COVID-19 does not discriminate relative to race, age, gender, status, education, or class. If you have fallen – this is your time to GET UP!!

As I write this, I realize the principles I taught years ago are even more prevalent now:

- Declutter Your Environment – order is a divine commandment. Set up a space that allows for creativity and positive thoughts to flow.
- Time Management – write down and be the guardian of time spent. Stay woke. Every moment is precious. Prior to the pause button, I didn't realize how much I was not accomplishing despite my best intentions. Minimize and eliminate activities that don't allow for the BEST YOU!
- Change Your Mindset – Covid-19 stress, fear and despairing thoughts are allowed, but don't let it consume you. Corona weight was on me! After gaining ten pounds in the first two months of the lockdown, I determined it was time for a mental shift. Just do it! 2020 could have been your worst year ever or the best year yet!
- Embrace Technology Change – Who would have ever predicted the pace of the shift as video-conferencing became the major communication source for businesses, schools, and churches to support working and learning from home. Analysts state the unprecedented adoption of cloud and video-based services that occurred in months would have taken years pre-covid. Welcome the "new norm", don't fight it!
- Be ready to PIVOT – if you stand still, you will get run over. The ability to transform may be your best survival skill amidst a pandemic.
- Create "ME" time and be still in the moment. Be sure to take the actions necessary to achieve financial, spiritual, health and self-development wellness.
  - o Financial Wellness – have a written plan for individual and business goals. Create a budget and track personal and business expenses. Successful individuals always understand their

money picture. Here is my testimony after applying a financial focus during the Covid-19 period:

- Increased personal FICO credit score by 80 points within 3 months.
- Developed a written plan and executed steps to create two additional streams of income.
- Reevaluation of monthly expenses via a "Wants vs Needs List" helped me identify unnecessary spending. I used the extra monies to add towards a six-month emergency savings fund.

o Spiritual Wellness – explore your spiritual core and operate in purpose. Always take time to meditate, express gratitude, and think positively.

o Health & Wellness – put a plan in place to ensure a sound physical, emotional, and social existence. Assess your well-being and remove relationships or habits that distract from living your best life.

o Self-Development – growth comes from learning. Invest in yourself continuously. Take online classes and challenge yourself to higher learning.

In essence, the secret to the sauce is this - in everything that you do, give back. Pay it forward. Share information. Use your knowledge and talents to help others. Blessings abound for those who do. The pandemic can either be an obstacle or a catalyst to propel you towards greatness. You decide. ARE YOU READY FOR THE CHANGE?

ABOUT THE AUTHOR
MICHELLE SENDERSON

Michelle Senderson is a mentor, motivator and coach focused on driving change. In parallel, she is a financial wellness expert and tax advisor with an extensive background in small business and individual tax deduction strategies.

Her passion lies in uplifting others and helping individuals win. She enjoys sharing the blueprint for successful, meaningful living that is serving and positively impacting lives. Waking moments are spent inspiring and empowering individuals with tips on how to make it through everyday life challenges. She equips individuals with information to become positive change elements for others.

WIDOW'S MEMOIRS

ANGELINA CROSBY-PIGOTT

My husband's name was Rudy M. Pigott; he lived and loved genuinely, possessed an unshakable faith in God, and expressed an unwavering love for his family and friends. He was the real thing. What you saw was what you got, no pretense, no ulterior motive, and no hidden agendas. While he considered himself shy, he could keep a conversation going with anyone with just a handful of words and a smile. Rudy's smile always preceded his arrival because his smile would light up the room. He was beautiful on the inside and out. He exuded love, joy, peace, patience, kindness, goodness, faithfulness, gentleness, and self-control in every situation. He was always calm under pressure and he was the voice of reason that kept our family grounded.

Rudy and I would joke about needing walkers to get around in during our golden years. Our dream was to retire, downsize to a two-seater, travel the world, and spoil our grand and great-grandchildren. On August 22nd, 2018, our plans intersected God's plan, and everything changed. August 30th, 2018 would have been our 15th wedding anniversary. I spent the next year and a half figuring out how to transition from "we" to "me" while trying to figure out widowhood and learning how to be a single parent again.

That was hard enough. I was already at capacity when the news of a COVID 19 pandemic broke; it was surreal. I prayed that it was just hyped-up fake news. However, my employer advising all non-essential employees to work remotely, and immediately closing the corporate office made it real. On top of everything that I was trying to navigate, now I would have to face a pandemic alone! Needless to say, I had no idea how to respond, so I freaked out. Rudy would have immediately gone into protection mode to ensure that our family would have what we needed to be safe.

My first response was fear, and my instinct told me to run. The initial plan was for my children and I to fly back home to St. Croix in the United States Virgin Islands to the safety of my extended family. There were numerous possible complications because of the unknown spread of the pandemic, and I was strongly advised against it.

My second response was to turn to the foundational beliefs that had gotten me through life's most challenging situations. Thus, I transitioned from a place of fear to a position of faith. I asked God for guidance, clarity, and direction on how to move forward. Immediately, God reminded me of the past experiences that I endured and overcame. God reminded me that I had never been alone because my family, longtime friends, and new friends had always been by my side, supported me, and helped me heal. Knowing that God would always protect and provide for my children and I and would never give us more than we could handle helped shift my perspective on how to respond to the COVID 19 Pandemic and my fears strategically.

With a newfound confidence, coupled with 20 years in Project Management & Project Controls experience, I devised a plan to prepare, provide for, and protect my family. I'm a researcher and planner by nature, so I got to work, and in response, I became somewhat of a prepper. As a result, I developed an "IF, THEN, WHAT" process, a tool I used to formulate a response to challenges. This process asks the question, "IF" _____ happens, "THEN" _____ could happen, so "WHAT" should I do now to prevent or mitigate the effect?

Here is an example. "IF" there was a food shortage and I could not purchase food from the grocery store, "THEN" my children and I could run out of food, so "WHAT" should I do now to prevent that from happening? In this scenario, my response would be to make sure that I had non-perishable food such as rice, grains, and dried beans on hand; ready to eat food such as canned vegetables, meats and grains; and other items like bottles of water and water filters, emergency cash, a back-up heat-source for cooking such as a camping stove, a full tank of gas in your vehicle, and other essentials.

Other situational responses that came up were how I would respond to an emergency where my children and I had to leave home in a hurry? It meant that we would have to have supplies packed so we could quickly grab them.

What about safety? I also had to consider having the means to protect my children and myself, such as a gun, a knife, or a baseball bat. Having something to protect my family and myself was imperative. In my case, I chose a Glock 19 9mm handgun and learned how to use it. I also ensured that my daughters, who were 17 at the time, attended gun safety classes and learned how to shoot.

Don't wait for another pandemic to put a plan in place to protect and provide for you and your loved ones. Consider doing the following; please note that this is not an exhaustive list, but it is intended to spark ideas.

- Conduct quarterly emergency drills at home.
- Keep your vehicle gas tank full at all times, never below a half tank.
- Have emergency cash on hand.
- Select a location outside the home where family members can meet during an emergency.
- Develop an emergency contact list, ensure that every family member has a printed copy, and place printed copies in all vehicles.
- Stock an emergency supply of shelf-stable food in the home if you had to shelter in place for an extended amount of time without power. Also include first aid kits, candles, batteries, a lighter or matches, bottles of water, water purification tablets or filters, and paper products.
- Consider packing the following emergency bags:
  - A 36-hour Bag: Keep this bag in your vehicle in the event of a roadside emergency. Include bottles of water, snacks, protein bars, a small first aid kit, flashlight, emergency contact list, flares or glow sticks, and a knife.
  - A 3-day bag: Pack a backpack for each family member if you have to leave home quickly. Include three days' worth of water, food, clothing, and essentials based on individual needs.
  - A Bug Out Bag: This bag should include things needed to survive for an extended period. Include non-perishable food that could be easily opened and eaten, a camping stove, utensils, a tarp, changes of clothes, blankets, a pop-up tent, and any other necessities that you could fit in the trunk of your vehicle that you can grab and go in 15 minutes or less. Also, have a plan for grabbing essential documents such as birth certificates, passports, insurance

policies, titles, deeds, and other important documents.

Being prepared is non-negotiable even under normal circumstances. However, there is a balance between being prepared and becoming obsessive that must be carefully weighed. While it is essential to stay informed, watching too much news could play a big part in manipulating how you respond. Unfortunately, you can't listen to everything being advertised as news. Relying on your faith in God and wise counsel is recommended. Know that God is with you always. When crisis hits, take stock of your life experiences and know that everything you need resides within.

My life is no longer dictated by fear and doubt. I am an overcomer, being made stronger and wiser through every experience. This is dedicated to Rudy M. Pigott, May 11, 1977 to August 22, 2018. As God continues to comfort us, Rudy's love will be the glue that binds us; his smile will keep us moving forward and our memories of him will keep us smiling.

ABOUT THE AUTHOR
ANGELINA CROSBY-PIGOTT

Angelina Crosby-Pigott, "The W.O.K.E. Strategist," is a project management & project controls expert, C.E.O., speaker, and author who uses her personal and professional experiences to empower others to elevate themselves. Angelina defines W.O.K.E. as a "Wise, Observant, Knowledge-seeker, pursuing Excellence."

Angelina empowers others to elevate themselves through "The W.O.K.E. Strategist" international conferences, her bestselling books, speaking engagements, strategic coaching sessions, and corporate consulting.

"The W.O.K.E. Strategist" is the summation of a woman who has lived a multifaceted life: (1) personally, as a teenage-mother, single-parent, wife, widow, ordained minister and former church planter, entrepreneur, and (2) professionally as a project management & project controls professional with over 20 years of experience in Cost Engineering, Cost Estimating, Planning & Scheduling in the Oil, Gas, and Nuclear Power industries.

Angelina's passion is to educate & to elevate by giving her clients the tools necessary to "Elevate Themselves" spiritually, mentally, physically, educationally, and economically while empowering them to rewrite their stories, build generational wealth, and create a legacy that is pressure-proof.

AN ENTREPRENEUR'S LIFE: THRIVING WHEN NO ONE ELSE IS GIVING YOU A JOB

OTHELIA SCHULTZ

What will life and business look like beyond 2020? This pandemic has already made history for the world, especially within America. Life as we knew it will never be what it was when we brought in the 2020 New Year. The children too young to realize the changes in how we live and do business will only read about what the world used to be like pre-pandemic. Everyone will be recounting the effects and how they survived this pandemic in their own family's history book. How have you dealt with family and friends during this time of social distancing? With over 500,000 deaths to date and counting here in the U.S. alone, how have so many dealt with the death of their loved ones?

To thrive amidst this pandemic, everybody must adjust to our new normal, and more importantly, create their own personal normal. COVID 19 wiped the slate clean for almost everybody. Everyone should look at this time as their new beginning and understand that we are all at the starting point on this very new and unfamiliar life path. It's not pleasant right now; no one was given an option on whether or not their life would change, but everyone has an opportunity to create what they want the rest of their life to look like.

Those fortunate enough to keep their jobs still had to make an adjustment in the way they do business; for the jobless, they had to make adjustments in every area of their lives. Many are challenged with how they will survive rather than thrive during this time. I will always be an advocate for entrepreneurship. I believe that is the only way to assure you have employment since you decide your value and you dictate your time. I have always told my children to make sure they have a way to make money if no one else will give you a job. Who knew a day would come that most of the country would be out of work?

I recently realized that entrepreneurship is in my DNA when I recalled stories about my grandmother. People would say she had million-dollar hands. She painted beautiful pictures, could knit or sew just about anything, then would take them to the local flea market and sell them as a way to make additional money. Growing up, my mom was always employed, but during the weekend she would do hair for extra money. She would also cook or bake and sell dinners to her coworkers at the hospital and nursing home. She hosted card game events and sold drinks and nachos. Eventually, mom decided to get her cosmetology license and opened her own beauty salon. It changed her life. She was free to make her own schedule and she had more time than ever to spend with the family. Although she was a natural giver and often gave more than what she charged, she determined what her services were worth and became quite successful.

I became an entrepreneur before I knew what it meant. I remember being about 6 years old and wanting to learn to braid hair so I could make money like my mom. I asked for a doll with long hair for Christmas and mom found me a black doll that I practiced on for what seemed like forever. I was about 9 years old when I made my first $5 for braiding my cousin's hair. Later, I was in middle school doing hair and makeup for classmates and friends on the days we had a dance or picture day.

They would have to buy me some candy or a drink at the dance, but that was of huge value back then. I continued in high school and upgraded my services to braids and extensions way before the rest of the world made it popular. I would cut the hair off my mother's old wigs and either sew them or braid them in because extensions as we know them now did not exist.

After high school, I went on to college to get certified in electronics and electronic assembly. Just before graduating, I met my husband who was in the military. When he got reassigned to a small town with no job opportunities in my field, I had to apply for any job that was hiring. Luckily, a friend told me to apply where she worked because they were hiring. Although I was the first applicant to arrive, I was told they already filled all the positions. Although I never experienced racism before, it was clear and blatant what the problem was. As I was leaving, I told my friend what happened, and she was as embarrassed as I was.

Those experiences quickly helped me decide that I not only needed a career that I could work wherever my husband would get stationed to, including overseas, but also that I needed a career that would allow me to work if no one else would give me a job. I needed to be able to stay at home and care for my young kids and my mother who was disabled, if necessary. I decided to follow what came naturally - cosmetology. I got my license, and my husband and I opened a beauty salon. After several years in the beauty salon, I decided to start a career in Real Estate to remain self-employed and control my own destiny. I continued to look for additional streams of income, becoming a serial entrepreneur selling Mary Kay, Tomboy

Tools, Body Magic, Quixtar, and the list goes on. These ventures were 2-fold. I was investing in things I was going to purchase anyway, then joined the company to get the "member discount." However, the added benefit was the potential to make money as well.

With so much uncertainty in the world, those who want to thrive amidst the pandemic should be intentionally making efforts to create stability in their careers and take the time to strategize for future generations. Now would be a great opportunity to teach the children our home life skills that are not taught in school, maybe a skill that can make them a little bit of side money as an entrepreneur like how to cook, bake, sew, do hair, or change a tire. These are all skills that my parents taught me, and my husband and I taught our children. I have no doubt that our kids are going to thrive during this pandemic. They were preparing for this their entire lives, starting when they were teenagers and had to cook a full meal once a week. They did it completely under protest, but they are excellent cooks now. We used to tell them, "Learn to do it yourself so you don't have to pay someone else." They do their own hair including barbering, they can and have repaired their own cars, they can rehab a home, and a long list of other marketable skills. They have the entrepreneurial spirit, but more importantly, these skills can help them save money or make ends meet if needed.

I don't know what my life will look like after the pandemic because my life has totally changed in spite of the pandemic, but my advice to anyone who wants to thrive in the midst of this pandemic is the same as what I have chosen to do. Get busy finding what interests you.

Get educated and creative in any way you can. Get online webinars or classes if they are affordable or free. If you have a lot of time on your hands due to Covid 19, take that time to create what you want your new normal to look like - a new hobby or a new career when the pandemic is over. Start working on those dreams or goals that your previous job commitment did not allow you the time to pursue. Sign up for anything that might help you gain knowledge in your area of interest. Join an online group or take some classes that force you to interact with other people in real time.

God willing, the pandemic will end soon, and we will all survive this. However, those who want to thrive during this time are going to have to make it a priority to be in tune with our changing way of life and proactively create their own opportunities for business moving forward beyond 2020.

ABOUT THE AUTHOR
OTHELIA SCHULTZ

Othelia Schultz is an entrepreneur, a self-starter and an educator who wants to motivate people to use their personal resources, be creative to improve their life, realize the strength and influence they have, and improve the lives of others in their family and their community.

Born Othelia Barbour, she was raised in a home where family values and religion were ever present her entire life. Her grandfather founded the first Church of God in Christ in New Jersey, and the church remains in the family as an icon in the community, as the street the church is on was dedicated to him in 2014.

Othelia spent most of her teenage years caring for disabled family members and is still today the guardian of one of them, who is now a disabled adult. Undecided on her passion, she decided to follow where the money was at and went on to a local college for a certification in electronics and electronics assembly. Just before graduation in 1996, she met a young soldier named Gregory Schultz who would soon become her husband.

Othelia has a long history in her community as a small business owner, an advocate in promoting efforts of other self-employed / entrepreneurs, and at times, an activist with extraordinarily strong views on equal rights. Othelia Schultz has been a Real Estate Broker since 2000.

In 2007 Othelia was also introduced to the National Association of Real Estate Brokers, the oldest minority trade organization in America, and in 2009, she founded Colorado Springs Realtist Association: NAREB's 97th chapter.

THRIVE

NIKKI CHEREE

Someone asked me how my people thrive during a pandemic
Because they can only see issues that are racist and systemic?
Patterns, processes, and rules that are in place
To make my people live in a place of pain and disgrace.
Is a pandemic a disease, or is it a threat to the whole?
Are they manmade creations to crush a person's soul?
My people have survived since the beginning of creation,
From turmoil and tragedies throughout every generation.
Yet they rise with resilience like a phoenix each time
With determination and strength that their ancestors left behind.
They don't worry about thriving but instead focus on how to live
In the world God created, and HE blessed them to give.
A helping hand, warm smile, and a loving touch
That enables the next man to stand when the going gets rough.
You see, to answer the question about how my people thrive,
One must only see things through spiritual eyes.
God never promised my people a life free from pain.
Through His shed blood, HE erased all guilt and shame,
Of being labeled less than human, underprivileged, or even leper
My people thrive through God's grace and standing together.

-Nikki Cheree

I find it ironic that the word "thrive" is a verb, and "pandemic" is an adjective. I want to bring to your attention that for a disease (which is a noun) to become a pandemic (worldwide spread of disease), it must take action (develop), which is, in essence, the very definition of the word thrive.

For a pandemic to thrive, a disease must become widespread in an environment of conducive hosts. The condition attaches itself to a place of nourishment, warmth, and in some cases, weakened immunity and takes up residence. May I suggest that you create a place of nourishment and warmth while strengthening the weakened immunity in your life? Do you see the connection?

I want to share with you two ways you can thrive during a pandemic. First, Change your Perspective. Second, Move with Intention. Let's talk about each of these further.

Change Your Perspective
During a pandemic, no one is exempt. I encourage you to step back and examine your frame of reference. Are you guided by fear or optimism about the future? A part of changing your perspective requires you to challenge your innate point of view.

The following are some ways you can examine how you see the world. Ask yourself:

Have I taken inventory of what matters to me the most?
Am I present in the moment?
Is love an action, or is it just a word?
How often do I slow down, breathe, and take in the sun?
Am I enjoying where I am in my journey?
Am I nourished by the diversity that life brings?

Answer those questions with honesty and see a new way of viewing life, even during unprecedented times. Living during a pandemic may force you to revert to the basics and rely on your five basic senses (sight, touch, taste, hearing, and smell). By doing so, you may see that your viewpoint has a lot to do with your ability to thrive instinctively.

Sight

I lost my godfather to COVID-19, and for the first time, I saw who my dad really was. My biological father was not consistent in my life, but he surfaced damaged, broken, and in need of help during the crisis. I came to understand the frailty of the man who planted the seed in my mom's womb, and God gave me the grace to repair the breach. I saw that in these unprecedented times, love was an action word. As I mourned the loss of one man, I gained a relationship with another.

Touch

There was a longing on the inside of me I never knew existed until the pandemic: the loving, warm, and protective touch of an embrace. The virus prohibited touch. When my mom was sick from COVID-19 and suffered from pneumonia, I could not touch her, hug her, and tell her everything would be okay. God, however, visited her room, and HE touched her. Just one touch by the Master's hands turned her life around.

Taste

How many people choose to focus on the basics? In the United States, I believe we had a taste of the good life: credit, excess, and no rules. The country was shaken to the core when the creature comforts were snatched away. We had to realize that our normal had changed in an instant.

The pandemic forced me to reflect. I "tasted" what my mom's life was like growing up in simpler times. My family ate at home and sat together for dinner. The pounds piled on because the comfort food nourished my soul. Everything tastes better with love when you slow down and are present in the moment.

Hear

I love the scripture that says, "Faith comes by hearing and hearing by the Word of God" (Romans 10:17). During the pandemic, God instructed me to listen and obey. He had work for me to do, but I had to stop listening to the negativity surrounding me daily.

I learned that hearing may not always be audible. It can also mean to perceive, be aware of, know of the existence of (Online Dictionary). Sometimes you must choose to eliminate the clamoring in your ear so you can get to the still, quiet voice that says, "Eliminate the people who are haters, fakers, takers, and waiters. They come to distract you with judgment and doubt." I spoke aloud the confirming words needed to motivate me to move forward and change my current situation.

Thriving should not be just about your ability to survive. What unspoken words have you heard that were matters of the heart that only you could solve?

Smell

What connection does smell have in terms of thriving during a pandemic? One of the common symptoms of Coronavirus affects a person's ability to smell. Smell is an important defense mechanism. It can, for example, alert you to foul odors or when something is burning. During a pandemic, we must follow the smell test and watch for the warning signs. Wearing a mask is necessary to protect your nose (smell). The nose is extremely sensitive. I liken it to being sensitive in the spirit and knowing how to protect what matters most.

Move With Intention

One of my favorite mottos is, "You have to do something to move something." I work with women and help them realize their potential. That means, have faith to pursue the impossible, have the purpose of taking deliberate action, and harness the passion for sustaining the journey. Do not be afraid of failure. The seeds you have sown will come to harvest if you faint not. To thrive, you must get back up again when you fail. Remain consistent in other aspects of your life where you spend most of your time (work and business).

Get Back Up Again

Even in the most desperate times, I followed the principles. I remained consistent. I had a budget and a plan. I have another motto: "Small steps make giant leaps." New beginnings can be a blessing in disguise. People often dread starting over, but I have learned that you can become focused and learn discipline in failure. In failure, you build muscle and stamina, and you learn obedience. No one can take your journey or process. The inner conflict you can overcome will set you up to make choices that can change your life's trajectory.

Double Down on the Job & Business

The same principles apply at work or in your business. When you think of thriving, you must also think outside of the home. God showed me overwhelming favor when I was willing to step outside of fear. I took on a new role and a new team during the pandemic. However, when racial tensions reached an all-time high with the death of George Floyd, executives came to me to help find a pathway forward for our employees. I could have stayed stuck or trapped by my own feelings of anger, hurt, confusion, and despair in those tense moments. Instead, I chose to be a vessel to bring hope in a dire situation.

Examine the questions like the ones below to see where you stepped up on behalf of your peers, teams, employees, etc.

- When did you say yes to something new and unconventional?
- Have you reimagined what is normal?
- How do you create a safe place for your team?
- How have you led from the heart?

- In what ways have you inspired people to adapt?
- What problems have you helped to solve?

During unprecedented times, there is no limit to what you can accomplish. Amid a pandemic, I was blessed beyond measure in every area of my life. Even during a crisis, you are exactly where God wants you to be. What will you do to make the most out of this season? The change starts within you!

ABOUT THE AUTHOR
NIKKI CHEREE

Nikki Cheree, The Corporate MC™, is a certified life coach, author, and financial literacy consultant. She is also a corporate executive with over 17 years of experience in human resources. It is this experience that makes her a phenomenal resource for elevating the business, brand, and lifestyle of every client she encounters.

In the corporate sector, Nikki Cheree has worked with Fortune 500 companies, and is instrumental in successfully leading multiple teams all over the US. She has been proven in her HR career through her numerous awards, including recognition from the Society of Human Resource Management where she obtained her certification as a Professional. Nikki Cheree currently holds expertise in the areas of Training and Development, Talent Management, Change Management, and Diversity Leadership. She currently holds a BS in Business Administration from The Ohio State University and a Master of Business Administration from Louisiana State University.

Nikki Cheree is a much sought-after coach and motivational speaker. She has shared her wisdom and experience through her "From Pain 2 Passion" workshops on platforms all over the country. Nikki Cheree is the author of "CONQUEROR!" a book she wrote to motivate you to jump over the hurdles of fear, doubt and stagnation that keep you from reaching your full potential.

Nikki Cheree believes *"You've got to do something to move something!"* and that's exactly what she does in every assignment to which she's called. She inspires others to move past what they deem to be setbacks and use them as advantages to overcome objections and self-doubt to ultimately attain every goal they've set for themselves.

IT TOOK COVID TO OPEN MY EYES

DIANNE BOWDARY

For years, the everyday grind and hustle fueled my mornings. I had places to go, people to see, and things to do. There was never enough time to get it done. I relished in the business of it all. My mornings started at 5 AM, and my nights ended at midnight. To-do lists, schedules, and regimens ruled my days. My travel schedule was so busy, in fact, that I was barely home long enough to enjoy my wonderful family or our beautiful home. Seattle, DC, Little Rock, Denver, Nashville, New Jersey, New Orleans, Dallas, Chicago, Philadelphia, LA - you name it, and I was there.

Both my husband and I are workaholics to a fault. We thrive on being at the top of our game. In the most recent years, I found myself working with the best bosses I have ever had in the most fulfilling jobs. The positions allowed me to partner with intelligent, powerful decision-makers in the healthcare industry. I was elated to bring value to my customers and my team. I loved the challenge of it all and viewed each day as a new adventure.

In the blink of an eye, it felt as though everything around me moved in slow motion. It was as if the earth stopped rotating on its axis, and all of life froze. We learned that people from other countries were infected with COVID-19 and were rushed to the ICU. Many had to go on ventilators and were sick indefinitely. By the time we learned of the infections spreading in the US, the death toll had become surreal.

The pandemic's enormity hit home when we heard of our own friends and neighbors who had tragic endings. City by city, everything and everyone but the essential personnel seemed to have shelter at home orders. Eventually, our jobs told us, "no more travel until further notice." Our healthcare systems seemed overwhelmed with COVID-19 cases. Oil and gas, retail stores, restaurants, airlines, and beauty salons were all reduced to a bare minimum at the mercy of this virus. Everyone was trying to figure this thing out.

Friends and colleagues were losing employment benefits and getting pay cuts. Even more friends were getting furloughed and laid off. I vividly remember waking up in the middle of the night, wondering when it would happen to us. I'd built up so much anxiety about losing our jobs that I couldn't sleep. My heart would start to palpitate stronger and more frequent. Every day I went down a new rabbit hole of what-ifs.

Several weeks passed, and my husband and I decided to develop an emergency plan. We never imagined that we could lose our jobs simultaneously, but it was happening all around us. We started looking into our emergency funds and tried to determine how fast we could access our money. My anxiety over the pandemic led me to obsess about our finances. We spent our evenings, weekends, and time off researching and studying all things money. We did not want to risk losing our retirement, home, cars, or anything that we worked so hard to build. In the process of our research, we came across His and Her Money on YouTube. They were featuring Dr. Lynn Richardson, financial guru and money mogul to the stars.

Let me tell you that after the first video, I was hooked. I immediately started reading everything I could get my hands on. I studied strategies around debt reduction, growing your money, and generational wealth. I took tons of classes and watched countless videos. I learned about the importance of spending less money, getting multiple streams of income, and getting back as much money back as the law would allow through my tax returns.

One of the game-changing lessons from New Wealth University was to track our spending. We did this in the past, but we weren't tracking the small stuff. As Dr. Lynn said many times, "Inspect what you expect." How could we expect to be debt-free millionaires, much less survive a pandemic, if we didn't know where our money was going?

And so, the inspection began. The list generator in me wrote down everything I was purchasing each month. I put a checkmark on the money that could be redirected to our "out of work" fund.

- There was the gym membership that I started in January and hardly used. *Check.*
- There was the dry-cleaning bill for all my work clothes. *Check.*
- Eating out about 5 days a week. So embarrassing. *Check.*
- Nights at the movies. *Check.*
- Valet parking. *Check.*
- Our wonderful vacations locally and abroad. *Check.*
- The numerous trips to the dog groomers, doggie daycare, and overnight boarding. *Check.*
- The weekly trips to the hair and nail salons. Ouch. *Check.*
- The massage therapist, as infrequent as those visits were. Sigh. *Check.*

- The weekly deliveries from online shopping. They were such good deals. *Check.*
- The countless things that I didn't need or forgot I'd purchased. *Check.*

I totaled the items that had a checkmark by them and wrote it down on paper. The amount I was spending each month was ridiculous. I multiplied that number by 12 months and almost passed out. I thought I was doing good with my spending. Each item on the list was reasonably priced, but what happens is every penny, every nickel, every dollar adds up. Who knew, all this time, when I thought I was controlling my money, my money was controlling me.

In contrast, when I am at work, I am acutely aware of every dollar spent and every dollar received for every product and service. In the role of sales, we must know our numbers inside and out. We are corporate entrepreneurs responsible for growing revenue while remaining fiscally responsible for our companies and our customers. I was proud of my mastery of the numbers and my ability to do right by the customer. If someone told me that my first job was to manage my home life like I run my business life, I would have been fired years ago.

And then it hit me. A eureka moment indeed! We need to track our expenses, and not just for the out-of-work fund, but as a normal course of business. We need to track our income. We need to develop more than one stream of income. We need to run our home like a business. We need a Family Income Statement, a Profit and Loss Statement, and all the other financial documents that apply. Our attention to detail, work ethic, and mastery over creating efficiencies and automated systems needed to be replicated at home. We needed to create a self-sustaining profit center at our home.

It's amazing how the information in the classes, the books, and the videos all start to come together when you apply it to your life. You don't have to live in fear of how you will survive financially anymore. The world needs to know that everyone should get a home-based business and run their life like a business. Not only is it possible to withstand whatever the future brings, but we can start to build wealth for ourselves and our families for generations to come. Dr. Lynn Richardson had been preaching this for years. It took a pandemic for me to hear and receive it. I grew excited at this revelation and I wanted to yell in exhortation. I'm compelled to motivate, inspire, and bring to the forefront how to apply these lessons to your lives and thrive in any condition.

And why is this so important right now? When the next life-changing event hits, be it a pandemic, a recession, a depression, or a local/foreign threat, you want to be financially prepared to deal with whatever comes your way. When you're not obsessed and worried about how your family will survive financially, it becomes much easier to focus on what's invaluable in life. I dropped the ball and lost my faith. I took everyone and everything that mattered for granted.

Hence, the most critical lesson of thriving amidst a pandemic is to know what's most important in life. For me, this was my relationship with God, my physical and emotional health, my relationship with my husband, family, and friends. Once you remember what's most important, we have to express it so that our loved ones know and feel it. Living these principles in your life will bring you peace of mind and a level of freedom that will blow you away. Number one is to respect the value of time because that's one thing that we can never get back when spent. I spent so many years being absent, both physically and emotionally, that I couldn't fully appreciate what was right under my nose. A beautiful marriage and a home filled with love. I slowed down long enough to embrace my surroundings like I was experiencing them for the first time. I had conversations with God like I never had before. I focused on my physical and emotional health and my relationship with my family and friends.

The impact has created an awakening in my life and a sense of presence that I have never had before. It has been so life altering that I am compelled to share this message with everyone within the sound of my voice. I am now a business partner with Dr. Lynn Richardson. Before, I was reading the lessons, but now, I have lived them. Each day brings a new message, but the core remains the same.

Be encouraged. When you run your life like a business and spend time with what's most important, your life will rise to the level of freedom and peace of mind that will sustain the tests of time.

ABOUT THE AUTHOR
DIANNE BOWDARY

Dianne Bowdary is a corporate executive, author, speaker, financial literacy coach, and performance improvement mentor. She is a master of leveling up human resources in others so they can achieve their greatest potential. Dianne is an authentic accountability coach, and she will not give up on you.

Dianne has over 20 years of experience in leadership roles in both Fortune 500 companies and startups. She maximizes her expertise to help others who want to get hired and get their money right.

Dianne and her family were born in the beautiful country of Belize and they moved to Chicago when she was 7 years old. She moved to Milwaukee to attend Averno College for Women and the University of Wisconsin, where she achieved her Bachelor of Science in Biology.

Dianne has worked in many fields, including Customer Service for a medical laboratory, lab management, as well as management and leadership roles within a Fortune 500 company. She has also been an entrepreneur, working with many others who had been laid off shortly after her own layoff.

She is passionate to help others thrive in their work environment and manage their money so that they will never experience another dire situation. Her purpose is to equip everyone with the tools needed to reach their absolute best potential.

SHIFTING UNAPOLOGETICALLY

ANDREA L. HAYDEN

In just a matter of months, life as we once knew it changed forever. The "2020 pandemic" profoundly reshaped our nation causing the entire world to watch virtually. The society that cares more about money than people has been shattered, forcing us to face some harsh realities while challenging our mindset personally and socially.

The collide created a perfect storm amid a worldwide pandemic that affected everyone the same regardless of income bracket, race, education, political affiliation, or religion. We were then thrust into an introspective state and self-realization, which can be frightening and debilitating to anyone. However, even though we have been affected the same, some of us will emerge better post pandemic than prior because of the willingness to shift mentally, pivot with a plan, and dig deep into untapped potential.

Fortunately, we have been given free will to choose how we personally view, navigate, and arise from life crisis. As the saying goes: "life is 10% what happens to you and 90% how you react, respond, and recover." Nevertheless, the emotional weight of coping and adapting in the attempt to thrive is enormous. I genuinely believe God is forcing the world to sit our butts down and reset our lives.

Personally, I have decided to receive this blessing, gift wrapped in a curse called "COVID19," as an opportunity to shift my life unapologetically! The Chinese definition of "crisis" is composed of two characters, one represents "danger" and the other "opportunity." I have termed this defining time in history as the gift of freedom. We have permission to radically redefine our lives and the definition of success without the care of scrutiny or judgment of others.

What is known for sure, as Oprah says, I do not want to return back to pre-pandemic life. Do not get me wrong, do I miss seeing and loving on friends and family, reopening my business, going to restaurants, dressing up and being free to move about without wearing a face mask…ABSOLUTELY!

This new taste of freedom and heightened awareness has enabled us to become more intentional and engaged with our families, discovering healthy habits and a new appreciation for the simple things like rest and relaxation, purging our homes, excercising and cooking regularly. The notion of the American dream has kept us disengaged from our families, exhausted, overwhelmed, burned out and completely out of balance.

As an entrepreneur of 28 years, a leader in the beauty industry, and a black woman in America, I fully own and understand the self-created condition of "misunderstood strength." The reality is that the calvary is not coming to save us. We must send out an **S.O.S…Save Our Selves**! I will no longer accept the pressures of being everything to everyone in the form of emotional labor. I have spent a great deal of my life giving my all to others, but have decided to keep some for myself. I challenge you to consider doing the same.

Some may find the task of self-mastery and re-imagining their new normal difficult, opting to accept their current situation and remain crippled by fear of the pandemic unknowns. No, it will not be easy, but neither is living in a constant state of stress and anxiety. You are miserably working a job that does not value you or serve your purpose, spending limited quality time with your family, trying to please others, and dumbing down your own goals. In addition, you lack time for self-development, deny your self-care, become emotionally exhausted and never seemingly obtain financial freedom.

I know some may think they would rather keep the devil they know instead of the one they do not know. However, I would dare anyone to change this narrative and turn that fear into focus, stay in position, and do not give up! This divine opportunity has exposed that our power is not wrapped up in possessions, but rather in who we are internally. In other words, we are enough! God designed us with a multitude of talents, passions, and the protected space reserved for our divine assignment. This has nothing to do with religion but has everything to do with how you show up in the world in service to others that is embedded in the DNA of your life's purpose.

We have been given a once in a lifetime do-over; it is now or never! The opportunity is now to lose the secret shame of past mistakes by getting beyond the labels that have falsely defined us. It is imperative to operate in and around people and things that empower us, especially post-pandemic. You must humbly seek relationships that inspire you to be better than you showed up. Positive connections are the new currency.

However, this will require changing some of your relationships. Bless and release the toxic, blood sucking haters and nay-sayers out of your life, understanding this may include family! This will allow you to trust yourself again and discontinue codependent relationships. Now, the real soul work can begin. Take the deep dive needed to analyze yourself and look within to find the courage and confidence to level up and transform ideas into reality. No matter what happens, we need to commit to taking action. Otherwise, we get stuck in the quicksand of self-doubt, disappointment, and fear, which I have experienced firsthand.

We must acknowledge the gravity of life as it happens, remembering action does not have to be perfect, just authentic. Along the way in your discovery process, you may uncover some new realities, such as your household could survive and thrive on one income in exchange for a family balanced life. Others may discover they possess everything required to become an entrepreneur using their amazing gifts and talents. A little-known fact, most people are already offering up goods and services. They are just not being paid for them!

During this COVID downtime, many have already decided on the freedom lifestyle, choosing experiences over the accumulation of things. Doing what you love in service of others allows you to live life with a renewed urgency. Imagine your next act being your best act. It is time to bet on YOU! It is time to reevaluate what makes you happy, thereby enabling you to dream wildly and achieve what was once considered impossible because of our over -burdened life.

Being happy does not require things to be perfect, it just requires you to look past the imperfections. Include this saying in your daily prayer; "Do not let anything stop me, especially me!" I believe this pandemic has come to shake things up, break the chains of bondage to people and things, expose our contentment with living happily with old victories and past successes, and having the audacity to think we are guaranteed the time to get it right.

I have been abundantly blessed to work within my creative passion for 39 years, receiving numerous accolades and recognitions. But it saddens me to think about the time I have wasted running, hiding, shrinking back, and playing small for years to avoid the bright lights of my life's deeper purpose. I became stuck in the middle passage, which is the space between where you were in life and where you should be. Everything has a beginning and an end. The middle is where people drown or remain in a miserable sunken place. By design, we are here to exponentially fulfill our purpose. By continuing to ignore the whispers, you become miserable and un-inspired with everything you have outgrown around you.

I have spent the last months reexamining my life. I had to come to the realization that this journey was about me, but not at all for me. Your journey should inspire others who are struggling and feeling hopeless. You may never know whose life you may impact, influence, or save. Just remain committed and continue walking blindly in faith.

It feels strange to say I am thankful for this pandemic because of the tragic events many have suffered. I would have never slowed life down long enough to confront and challenge my past and future self. I have literally spent my entire working life doing what I love. Starting at the age of 16, I have enjoyed helping women feel courageous, confident, and beautiful; and currently, I specialize in empowering women suffering silently from hair loss. I realized that God had abundantly blessed my mind as He had my creative hands. I have the gift that many people seek to transform their ideas into action, turn fear into funnels of possibilities, and enable them to bank their brilliance.

Unbeknownst to me, this created a bright light over my life that others could see, but I continued to deny for years. I was allowing others to eat freely from the fruits of my labor. Meanwhile, I suffered from perfectionism and achievement-phobia! The pandemic disruption allowed self–inflicted fear to set in. It also granted me the mental clarity to realize that my value and strength expanded well beyond the chair. Little did I know, the 2020 pandemic would begin the season of hard decisions and transformational growth that would stretch me past any recognizable point of comfort. You see, God knew it would take a worldwide pandemic to make me stop, listen, re-focus and radically shift and move forward.

We all can recreate our life and establish new non-negotiables. The call for me to pivot into position was loud and clear. I will no longer keep these gifts as secrets and side hustles, nor will I offer them as emotional labor. My purpose is to reach, teach, connect, and incite action with other women in various ways as the COVID-19 pandemic continues to propel small businesses and solopreneurs into new realities.

By no means do I proclaim to know or have it all together. We are all a work in progress, just in different stages. I challenge you to end what is blocking your ability to move forward, stop the negative self-talk and trust your intuition. In these uncertain times, you have no more time to waste. Let us get to work and know this: the only thing stopping you is you!

ABOUT THE AUTHOR
ANDREA HAYDEN

Andrea Hayden, founder of The Hair Management Group, has 39 years in the Cosmetology, Hair Restoration, and Trichology industry. Essence magazine listed her as one of seven hair loss experts in the country. As the past Director for the International Association of Trichologists USA, she oversaw all operations, which included establishing the U.S based World Trichology Conference. Andrea uses her resources and network to connect professionals that often lead to business collaborations.

Andrea has built an enterprise that helps women reach the medical and nutritional support to restore their self-esteem while managing their hair loss. Andrea governs the treatments for hair loss clients and training seminars for licensed cosmetologists and trichologists. Andrea is sought after for her business acumen. She provides guidance on event planning, website development, marketing design, space planning, contract negotiations, private labeling human hair attachments, plus assisting stylists and trichologists in recession proofing their businesses. Andrea uses her resources to keep beauty and hair loss professionals aware of the ever-changing COVID-19 landscape, while assisting others in securing business funding, community grants, and other resources to save their small businesses.

She was named an ambassador of the southwest region for The National Hair Society and is a volunteer with the American Cancer Society. Andrea was awarded The Marlene Hansen Award from the International Association of Trichologists and was the San Antonio Business Journal recipient of the Women's Leadership Award for Inspirational Leadership.

NEW NORMS

DR. VANESSA DE DANZINE

COVID-19, notably known as the coronavirus, creeped upon us unannounced like a thief in the night. A sure testament that life is short and not promised. Colorless and odorless with a fierce speed of power that took innocent lives. Who were the weak? The elderly, the immuno-compromised, and those victimized by systemic racism. A system working how it is designed to work. Following the news across chartered waters, I sat at home in Panama when reality hit: we are in a pandemic. My son and his family left 2 weeks before the first case in Panama, but only to return to New York, the epicenter. I felt helpless, but I knew I had to stay informed with updates, since kids don't really follow the news. I was surrounded by some family, but the majority of the kids were in New York. The challenge to seek alternatives to boost the immune system caused me to resort to old school remedies.

While life and death were on a chess board, the vision of money became a strategic tool. I thought, who can think of money at a time like this? I began to follow Dr. Lynn Richardson's New Wealth University after supporting a colleague who sent me her link as a financial consultant. Where was Dr. Lynn 20 years ago? My life would definitely be different today, but it's never too late. There was an epiphany to detour COVID and focus on changing the mindset of everyday challenges. It wasn't just watching videos of Dr. Lynn; it was when she called me in Panama, and when I heard the passion in her voice, I knew this was my pawn on the chess board. Although the books arrived in New York, my son and daughter-in-law were not just screenshotting the pages, they were also reading the books before they sent them to me. They were my first students. I started reaching out to friends and family who became fascinated with the new knowledge and were eager to learn more. I knew my daughter could also benefit. I thought this was going to be a challenge for me to convince her, but to my surprise, she jumped right into the Entrepreneur's Academy. It wasn't just about making money, it also highlighted lessons learned about life yielding to a new norm. Under the auspice of New Wealth University, I became a Wealth Ambassador. I'm on the bandwagon of not just learning financial consultancy, but financial coaching, how to start a homebased business, how to hire your kids, building multiple streams of income to create generational wealth, crafting a master achievement plan, and learning how to get my money back by learning the rules of the game then playing the game by their rules. Now, I am a member of the Speaker's Bureau and am learning about the stock market; I'm unstoppable.

Convincing people to spend less money is a challenge. Some who can visually see it, can appreciate it. Those who I have to keep talking to until they're blue in the face obviously don't get it, but I keep trying. Some look at me as if I'm saying something foreign when I tell them: learn how to manage your money and not let your money micromanage you. A simple concept taken recklessly out of context. Dr. Lynn's strategic breakdown provides structure and flexibility for those struggling financially but want to change their mindset. COVID was the light bulb for some who became crippled and paralyzed when they realized they had no savings and were at the mercy of survival.

Overnight, unemployment soared the alarm to a wake-up call. Although retired, having a home-based business and building multiple streams of income has put others on the path to control. I started building my empire by starting a home-based business, and I am currently focusing on expanding my real estate network to build those multiple streams of income. I'm more organized, taking classes, and becoming more self-disciplined. Knowing that many jobs will not return, I echoed these trainings to teach others to be self-disciplined. I stress to others the importance of Annuities, IRAs and creating a pension for themselves.

I've worked around death for decades only to witness individuals dying alone of COVID. However, it's never the same when it hits home. I laid my Mom to rest October 2019, and although we knew she was going to pass before she knew, my sister, brother and I made sure we were there until her last breath. When she had three weeks to live, I texted all the kids and they came with my niece and nephews. I speak of this because it was no better way for her to go but being surrounded by family and loved ones. I don't think I would be in my right mind if she was alone. I say that to say this: never take life for granted because when it's gone, it's gone. After learning about estate planning, it was evident that people didn't have their affairs in order. Although I was the representative for my mom's will, I learned the importance of a Trust even if you only have one child. Now, a Trust supersedes my Will. I could not reiterate it enough for people to get insurance with a Long-Term care provider. I turn blue in the face just hearing about the lack of basic insurance they have, but I have to keep following up.

I can talk for days, so much of me has evolved within a few months. When I have order and the strategic tools, I can protect my family and much more. I've become not just a pillar to my friends and family, but to the community. I have a due diligence to engage others on the path to financial freedom. A concept long overdue.

ABOUT THE AUTHOR
DR. VANESSA DE DANZINE

Dr. Vanessa Vielka de Danzine is a retired NYPD Detective encompassed with more than two decades of educational consultancy as a co-host, speaker, trainer, author, journalist, community advocate and financial literacy consultant: a collective symphony coupled to her vast array of leadership skills to help underserved communities build wealth.

As an honoree, a Diamond W.E.A.L.T.H Ambassador partnered with Dr. Lynn Richardson on a shared parallel platform, Dr. de Danzine is able to teach, educate and lead others to pivot into the mindset of financial freedom to create and build generational wealth. A vetted leader as Director, Community Based Organization Partners-BK, Past Chair, Community Based Public Health Caucus, an affiliate of the American Public Health Association and Past President, and National Community Based Organization Network, she has paved the pathway to bridge intersections of community and finance towards financial freedom.

Dr. de Danzine is a fearless pillar in the community focused to untap the inner fears and promote the paradigm of spending less money, getting more money, and foremost, getting your money back.

THE PARALLELS OF PANDEMIC FINANCES

VIRGIE M. BULLIE

During his December 2, 2020 interview with the U.S. Chamber of Commerce Foundation, Dr. Robert Redfield, Director of Centers for Disease Control & Prevention (CDC), answered, "this nation was severely underprepared for this pandemic," and he "wasn't prepared to understand how little investment had been made in the core capabilities of public health at what is the premier health institute in our nation. We really have not invested where we need to be in day-to-day analytics and predictive data analysis. We really haven't invested in what I call laboratory resilience - to make sure that our public health capacity has multiple platforms."

Question: Do you think our experiences [as a nation] with Covid-19 will prepare us for the next crisis which is bound to come? During the most devasting infectious disease pandemic since the measles, the nation's lack of investment in the CDC, the country's leading public health organization, continues to cause collateral damage of fatal proportions. It leads me to believe that no matter the environment, the ill-prepared will at some point experience devastation in their personal financial situations. Conversely, some say Billionaires, Millionaires, or Witnesses will be born out of this crisis. Which will you become?

How can this be?

Whether it is the government or U.S. citizens, a DECISION was made to inadequately fund the CDC or one's personal savings. To avoid your budget shortage, there are few steps you must note. Starting today, you must track every dollar earned and every dollar spent. Daily tracking of your day-to-day expenses and analyzing your income and expenses from month to month will give you control of your money. At the end of the month's conclusion, you can predict the likelihood of the future outcome, a surplus or a deficit, based on historical data. You can determine needs (what is essential?) from your wants (what is non-essential?). Lack of investment in yourself creates self-doubt and issues with your confidence which can further impact your home, business, career, and your health.

Who is essential?

Covid-19, aka Coronavirus, has exposed our nation's implicit biases in our healthcare and education systems. The law of supply and demand exacerbated the prices of the "essential" items and our hospital systems were in jeopardy of providing top-shelf patient care for all. The Covid-19 Cares Act exemplified the government's support toward business owners rather than the employees. Millions of taxpayers received a a few thousand dollars at best, whereas small businesses received hundreds of thousands of dollars from the Small Business Association (SBA via the Economic Injury Disaster Loan (EIDL) grant and loan programs and the Paycheck Protection Program (PPP) program. These programs highly favored business owners, including sole proprietors, independent contractors (1099 wage earners), freelance workers, and those with homebased businesses.

Many households have had to face tough decisions as they

suffered job and human losses. Unemployment applications topped over 41 million and at one point, over 21 million people had not returned to work. Businesses have lost employees and revenue. Families have lost loved ones and income. To endure, households have had to reconcile personal and household expenses. Families are choosing to replace cable with streaming services and preparing family meals vs. eating out.

In many cases, individuals and families are making do on unemployment (no additional income) or on one income, which is significantly lower than their Pre-Covid income. To that end, everyone must run their life like a business. Everyone should have a home-based business today. Many experts declare that we should have at least 9 streams of income, four of which should be passive income. This pandemic has knocked us upside our heads and helped us to understand, as Dr Lynn Richardson often shares, "One income is hazardous to our W.E.A.L.T.H!"

What can we do to minimize the negative impact of a pandemic?

- Wear your masks America!
- Do not congregate in enclosed spaces.
- Physical distance at least 6ft, at all times.
- Wash your hands.

These directives were highly suggested by the CDC, the World Health Organization, other medical associations, and world-renowned scientists. We cannot get 100% participation without clear consistent reinforced messages conveyed to the public. Therefore, we cannot mitigate this pandemic. Throughout this crisis, the true heroes & the essential workers have been revealed. Thank you for your determination and grit that you display daily to serve our nation.

In elementary school, we learn safety drills for a tornado, fire, earthquake, and sadly, active shooter drills. Many times, the children are encouraged to create a fire drill for their homes. Though we craft a set of plans for natural disasters, there is no plan at school or at home to prevent financial disasters.

Therefore, you must decide to invest in a financial education and teach your entire family. You must read, take classes and attend webinars; and guess what, you can do so from anywhere! (www.learnandearnwithlynnandvirgie.com)

NO EXCUSES!

Here's one thing we know for sure: People have had money problems in the past. People are having money problems in the present. People will have money problems in the future.

What can you do to minimize the negative impact of a financial crisis?

Put your **M.A.S.K.S.** into action every day!

- **M**ake more money!
- **A**lways live below your means!
- **S**chedule your money!
- **K**eep track of every penny daily!
- **S**tart a home-based business!

Lifechanging events like a pandemic will make you analyze your needs vs your wants. When your finances are stretched to the limit, you will begin to reevaluate how to make more money. Due to a loss of income, you can rely on your skill sets developed over the years. You can start a home-based business because as a business owner who runs your life like a business, you have access to hundreds of tax deductions as a sole proprietor.

Learn the lessons of the pandemic and allow them to propel you Beyond 2020. Determine your key essentials for survival and defend against infectious distractions. Develop a surgical thoughtful strategic plan that consistently produces multiple streams of income. Decide to properly manage your assets for your family and for future generations.

Decide to thrive . . . Beyond 2020.

ABOUT THE AUTHOR
VIRGIE M. BULLIE

Virgie M. Bullie is a woman of many talents with over 30 years in customer satisfaction experience. She began her career supporting local family-owned businesses at the Ann Arbor Credit Bureau and worked up to supporting 500 companies over her 30 plus years. Today, she owns Virtually 4 You and believes "if your chaos is not organized, then it's just chaos!"

When she is not keeping everyone around her organized, Virgie enjoys relaxing with friends, and giving back by advocating for others through public service as a member of Delta Sigma Theta Sorority, Inc. and current member and immediate past president of Jassac Charitable Foundation, Inc.

In 2016 after a companywide layoff at Computershare, Virgie became a partner in Brainpower Consulting, Inc. and Global 360's Executive Assistant to its CEO. Virgie makes sure the team is always on one accord.

Ms. Bullie studied Computer Science and Mathematics at Midland University and graduated with B.S. Mathematics with Minor in Computer Science from Eastern Michigan University.

Today she lives in Illinois where she is the president of the board of directors for her non-profit cooperative housing community of over 540 units, where she manages a multi-million-dollar budget.

TRANSFORMING YOURSELF TO PREPARE FOR THE POST PANDEMIC WORLD

DR. CATRINA PULLUM

We are living in a time where events have occurred that have not been seen in nearly 100 years. A force of nature has pushed us as a planet into our homes and shelters to review, reflect, study, and change. Almost all aspects of our society are altered in some form or fashion because of the Coronavirus pandemic. Hopefully, you have used this time to reflect on what you have accomplished in life so far and to start casting your vision of what your life will be in this new post pandemic world. You might ask, "Why do we need to do that?" So many aspects of life are changing from what we know, and it will be imperative to adapt to survive. Traveling, shopping, and working will all be different going forward. The good thing about this is with crisis comes opportunity. We need to start positioning ourselves to take advantage of the new opportunities that will come out of this new normal.

Accepting the Loss
As humans, we tend to strongly associate with and remember the bad memories more than the good ones. This attachment

to negative encounters is what forms the foundation of many of the chains that bind people today. The intensity of the memory will generally determine the strength of the chain. Understanding this, we see that intense, bad experiences turn into limitations on our present and our future. Accepting the loss means does not mean we excuse the horrible things that have happened, it means we understand that while what happened cannot change, we can rise anyway. Those events have a purpose in shaping who we are today. If we do not do this work, those experiences can become chains anchoring us down and placing limitations on our lives. We have to learn to use those events as fuel and a driving force in our lives. Embrace your past and love yourself, all of yourself, including the parts of you that went through the storm.

Realize that even though you went through the storm, you got tossed and turned around, you were muddied and soaking wet, and at times it was so dark you couldn't see your hand in front of your face, still, you came out the other side alive! James Baldwin once said, "Not everything that is faced can be changed, but nothing can be changed until it is faced!" Facing the events of your past and realizing that you came through them gives you the chance to do something more with the experience, other than remain trapped in it. Some things are gone, some for a short while, others for good. We should spend our energy focused on where we go from here, instead of trying to get things back that are gone. Once we come to terms with the fact that change has happened, we are then open to look at where we are now.

Assessing the Present
Assessing the present requires taking an honest, real inventory of yourself and where you stand in all aspects of your life. It's hard to plot a course if you don't know where you're starting from! You need to know your capabilities to form a plan on how to use them in the new normal. Assess all areas of your life: physical (where you live, your health), mental (your goals,

your dreams, your skills), emotional (your relationships with yourself, your family, your associates, and your friends), spiritual (what directs your moral compass, your faith and beliefs), and any other aspects of your life you deem important. Focus on two things: where are you now and where do you want to be?

There are some things you may have to let go of. There are things you may want to or need to start doing that you were not before. You might find that there are activities that dominate your life and bleed the time out of it. Or you might find that there are people doing the same thing, sucking the joy and energy out of your life, diminishing your ability to contribute to the world. Identify. Classify. Everyone has a purpose in life. There are things that you were brought into this world to accomplish that no one else can. You have to determine what those things are and position yourself to do that work. Taking an accurate inventory of your S.W.O.T. – strengths, weaknesses, opportunities, and threats – will position you to make the right moves in this new post pandemic world.

Ascertaining Your Future

Ascertaining your future today requires an analysis of how your assessment of yourself aligns with the opportunities developing from this crisis event. The analysis should show you the gaps you need to close between where you are and where the new opportunities will be. Use what you learn in the previous two steps, the lessons learned from your past and during your self-assessment, and with that information in hand, construct your plan on how to move forward Beyond 2020. Make a plan comprised of a number of short term/short range goals. Those goals should be focused on closing the gaps you identify.

Once you have a plan started, complete a vision building

exercise. Take the vision and record it in a format to remind yourself every time you see it what the plan is. It is said that the eyes are the window to the soul, so something visually appealing to the eye should quickly, at a glance, remind you of a message to your soul. An easy tool for this job is a vision board. A vision board is simply a poster board containing words, pictures, and images to remind us of the path we are supposed to be walking daily.

As you search for items to place on the vision board, listen for the call on your life. Get magazines, newspaper ads, any sources of words and pictures you are comfortable cutting up, and as you begin to leaf through them, listen to your heart. Listen for that still, small voice. Listen for what calls to you. You might find a picture of a doctor or a nurse, which causes your heart to leap. You might see a motorcycle and can hear the roar of the engine, which allows you to picture yourself out on the open road. You might see affirmative words like "hope," "love," "beautiful," "strength," "joy," "happiness," or "family." These words might speak to the chains you have recently broken in your life or resonate along a chain still waiting to be broken. Search for and find the things which call to you and speak to your destiny: to your calling. Paste, tape, glue, or draw, but record it all on the vision board: all that you have seen and heard for your life!

Our new normal is changing the way we function in the world. What opportunities will you take advantage of? Will you become an entrepreneur and start a new business? Or maybe you will facilitate the physical or digital delivery of goods and services? It's a brave new world out there. Don't get left behind! Accept, Assess, and Ascertain!

ABOUT THE AUTHOR
DR. CATRINA PULLUM

Dr Catrina Pullum is a Louisiana native making a global impact as **The Chain Breaker**. She is an entertainment executive & visionary who is known as "The Whisperer" in the industry. Dr. Catrina's life's mission is to help individuals walk in their purpose by creating, igniting, and influencing them to **Unleash and Embrace Their Power**. As a producer, she creates a platform for individuals to share their stories of triumph through the Arts.

Dr. Catrina serves as the Sr. Vice President of Artist & Talent Management and Operations for Sunni Gyrl, Inc. Dr. Catrina has been featured in Essence, O & Black Enterprise Magazines, to name a few. Dr. Catrina has received honors from President Barack Obama, Congress members, State Representatives, and others. Dr. Catrina's work has included working with the Now You See National Campaign, Just US organization, Junior League, Women In Film, and RAINN among other organizations and initiatives.

Through her philanthropic endeavors, Dr. Catrina is making a global impact through her active board membership for various charitable organizations.

PANDEMIC LESSONS

SYRENA N. WILLIAMS, MBA, JD

During the pandemic, everyone has had time to think: think about what they are doing, and what they would like to be doing. The time when we were normally driving to and from the office, or flying to and from work sites, we can now use to think about if we are really doing what our heart desires. It has taken the pandemic for some of us to realize that we are here for a purpose and we must live and walk in that purpose. For many of the people that I have spoken with, that purpose has included entrepreneurship. People have identified that they have an idea of a product or service that the world needs, and now with everyone intentionally connecting on the web each day, they can reach anyone who needs it.

Once someone has decided that they have a gift to give to the world, they immediately want to work on developing that idea and getting it to the people. Now is the time to pause and think about what it will take to make it happen.

1 - Assess what you need to bring your business to life and determine if you have what it takes to do that (time, money, skills, etc.). If not, develop a plan to acquire that and the people who you believe will support you.

2 - No one builds a business alone! Not a successful one. Think about what type of expertise you need and who has it.

- Do you have a business coach to assist with business structure needs (best legal entity, operating agreement, dissolution plan, resolutions, strategic planning, etc.)?
- Do you have a lawyer to help with legal needs (contracts, non-disclosure, regulations, etc.)?
- Do you have a financial guru to help with projections (profits, losses, understanding costs, etc.)?
- Do you have a CPA who can advise on your tax planning (tax status, write-offs, new rules, etc.)?
- Do you have a marketing person (social media, image, brand, etc.)?
- Do you have industry expert mentors (to help you learn the industry and learn from their mistakes)?

3 - Develop a realistic target for your launch and quarterly goals. How many people are you able to serve? What is your capacity?

Pause for a moment and think about where you want to be, and what it will take to get you there. If we were building a house, we would not be buying furniture before we discussed the foundational floor and walls of the house. Similarly, the structure is going to sustain you through the long haul as you change your look, brand, product and service delivery of your business. Build it right the first time!

Now, to tell the truth, no entrepreneur loves the administrative part of building and keeping a business going. And if you are already in the thick of things, know that there is nothing wrong with opening a sole proprietorship while in the developing stages, and testing your idea on your target market. This is actually a great idea. However, once you have pinpointed the direction you want to go in, and you have accessed your capacity to run the business (part-time or full-time), you need to make provisions to get your business affairs in order. Remember, this is not a hobby, it is a business! The key to being successful is knowing what you know and knowing what you do not know.

While this process is not the fun part, it is necessary to catapult you to your dreams. It is drive, determination and discipline that provides business owners with victory. Regular use of best practices generates habits that create protection for you and your business as you build and grow. Building a business the right way takes time, money, and resources. But remember, it is better to build it right than to have to tear it down and fix or rebuild the foundation.

ABOUT THE AUTHOR
SYRENA N. WILLIAMS

Syrena utilizes her educational experience gained from her MBA and JD, coupled with her work and life experiences, to assist individuals/organizations with every aspect of their business by providing powerful and perspective shifting interactions. This is delivered through custom legal services, individual coaching, workshops, facilitations, as well as speaking engagements.

Ms. Williams has over fifteen years of business planning, strategic planning, project management, networking, effectiveness and efficiency process training and facilitation experience. She has served as a consultant to several organizations providing extensive support with identifying goals, areas for improvement, and unresolved issues. She works to ensure strategies and techniques that advance the organization's missions and shareholder's interests. She specializes in long-term coaching and advising to provide protection for the client while providing proven results to clients while being discreet in her visibility. Ms. Williams' keen interest in helping her community develop and grow drives her work to arm others with relevant, timely information in order to maximize their ability to advocate for and achieve their own success. She has mentored numerous Black-owned fledgling businesses to improve their back-office processes and procedures. Her many roles with organizations have provided her an opportunity to utilize and grow varied skills sets to enhance the skills, goals and capabilities of others. Syrena Williams is the co-owner of CW Law Group, PLLC, she leads community and professional education classes through Practical Skills University, and she teaches entrepreneurship at NCCU School of Law. Ms. Williams is an active service member in her community of Durham, North Carolina.

BRAND PROTECTION PIVOT BEYOND 2020

MICHELLE J. MILLER, ESQ., LLM

"The most common way people give up their power is thinking they don't have any." – Alice Walker

To successfully pivot and thrive **Beyond 2020**, it's integral that you establish a proactive strategy for protecting your brand, your content, and your business. The economic impact of the global shutdown due to Covid-19 has wreaked havoc on businesses large and small. The economic impact of Covid-19 has resulted in a decrease in job opportunities. Still, it has also resulted in many people taking a leap of faith into entrepreneurship to provide for themselves and their families. Many have proclaimed an economic recession **Beyond 2020**, but this book gives you strategies for economic progression **Beyond 2020**.

Due to Covid-19, there has been a substantial increase in internet usage. As a result, the probability of business, content, and brand exposure has increased, making it easier for more people to come in contact with your products and services. The increase of time spent in the home due to Covid-19 has given people time to tap into their creativity resulting in new entrepreneurial ideas and business innovation. Protecting intellectual property is more important than ever during this time and **Beyond 2020**, especially since people are taking advantage of opportunities to infringe on intellectual property rights by copying designs, trademarks, or other works during the pandemic.

You must be proactive and not just reactive **Beyond 2020**. I get excited when clients call me before a product or service launch because I can help prevent future headaches by putting the proper legal strategies and documentation in place before any problems. If you didn't launch with a lawyer's assistance before 2020, you need to retain a lawyer's services, even if it's to identify legal gaps that increase your business risk.

A positive outcome of this increased exposure has resulted in increased money-making opportunities for some industries. A negative effect of this increased exposure is more people stealing brand names and content to make money. Covid-19 has caused many people to start businesses. Still, without a proactive intellectual property protection plan, a profitable company can virtually bankrupt if its owner has to obtain a lawyer to prove ownership of a brand that should've been protected before or when the owner launched the business.

As we have witnessed in 2020 courageously, everything has changed and will continue to change in 2021 and beyond. In prior decades, a business's value was primarily based on its tangible assets (property, equipment, inventories, etc.), but this changed dramatically around 2010. In 2010, people filed over 200,000 trademark applications with the United States Patent and Trademark Office (USPTO). In 2019, that number increased to over 400,000 applications. Now, intangible assets (patents, trademarks, copyrights & trade secrets) account for a significant part of business valuation, and I believe this will continue **Beyond 2020**. The days of only protecting your tangible business assets are over; it's essential to safeguard your intangible business assets as well – your intellectual property. Your intellectual property includes the following:

- Trademarks
- Copyrights
- Trade Secrets
- Patents

People often mix up the purpose of each component of intellectual property. Here is a simple way to know the difference, without all of the legal nuances:

- a *trademark* as a name, logo, slogan, and/or other unique identifiers used to sell products and/or services;
- a *copyright* is an original creative work;
- a *trade secret* is economically valuable secret company information; and
- a *patent* is a process, design, or invention.

The purpose of intellectual property rights is to encourage new creations, including new books, music, technology, artwork, inventions, and other forms of expression that might increase economic growth. The survival of entrepreneurial endeavors and companies' existence depends on their ownership and control of their intellectual property. Business **Beyond 2020** requires ownership of your intellectual property, especially since there has been a significant societal shift in computer activity due to Covid-19.

Because of the pandemic, people rely heavily on e-learning and e-commerce due to social distancing, so online activity has increased. Because of online activity, criminals are seizing opportunities to make fast cash through the sale of counterfeit products, and opportunists are creating new names and services in the marketplace by stealing brands and copying content. One pivot you must make due to the pandemic is to shift from being a company employee to a company owner. The sudden and unexpected loss of employment left people in distress, but if you want to experience progress and profits **Beyond 2020**, you must do the following:

1. Start a new business or another business;
2. Obtain the appropriate legal contracts for use in your business;
3. Identify your business assets, both tangible and intangible; and
4. Protect your business assets by protecting your real property and intellectual property.

My law office, The M. J. MILLER Law Firm®, also known as The Digital General Counsel™, provides legal assistance for all of the above. A brand protection pivot is necessary to establish a sustainable path to profitability and enhance brand value in the minds of consumers who are being bombarded with business content online. In fact, an intellectual property pivot is needed **Beyond 2020**.

Counterfeiters, copycats, brand bandits, and content stealers create consumer confusion that destroys brand loyalty and damages reputations. Almost daily, I see people on social media complain about someone stealing content from their online courses, copying their coaching and speaking content, stealing their creative ideas, and stealing their brands. People complain as if they cannot control the use of their content and brand; they unconsciously relinquish their power by failing to protect their content and brands. I then see people chime in the comment section proclaiming that these people can create something new.

Creating new things is wonderful. However, at some point, you need to stop creating and re-creating things that make you money simply because people keep stealing them. At some point, you must decide to stop investing money in the creation of ideas that share and pitch in public, but don't protect. I also watch people launch new businesses without appropriate contracts in place and without protecting their brands. Wouldn't you like to have the peace of mind of knowing your brand and content are protected?

You can protect your new or continuing business and money-making opportunities from copycats and brand bandits by obtaining the highest level of legal protection possible for your intellectual property. The highest level of U.S. brand protection comes with the registration of your brand as a federal trademark. The highest level of U.S. content protection comes with making a federal claim for the content you create as a copyright.

If you offer products or services outside of the United States, you need an international intellectual property strategy. Due to the progress of technology and globalization in the 2000s, at first, only a few businesses needed to worry about national and international intellectual property protection. However, due to the substantial rise of e-commerce and internet activity, many entrepreneurs and companies are now almost instantly national and international, so intellectual property protection issues have become far more generally applicable and will continue to be so. In other words, **Beyond 2020**, you must protect your business, creative ideas, and brand on all sides.

After working with numerous entrepreneurs, ministry leaders, business owners, and celebrities, I realize that many people haven't identified their brand portfolio components and haven't identified all of their copyrights or trade secrets. Your first strategy for brand protection **Beyond 2020** is to conduct an internal brand protection audit or obtain a lawyer's services from someone like me to do it for you. During a brand protection audit, you must identify your brand portfolio's components. You must assess your current brand protection efforts, and you must create a prioritized list of everything that's unprotected and, therefore, at risk of theft. I recommend combining your brand protection audit with a copyright audit, a trade secrets audit, and an assessment of contracts.

Second, obtain a lawyer's services from someone like me to register and update all intellectual property rights, including in countries where your products are sold and/or where you consistently offer business services.

Third, you must perform online monitoring and capture evidence of infringement to exercise your right to have the content removed or taken down.

Fourth, you must monitor your protected intellectual property, including working with legal counsel to send cease and desist demands and to execute other strategies if the demands are not honored.

Finally, you need to have legal counsel review the contracts that you have in your business or that you have signed to determine if they impact your intellectual property rights and if so, how. As a lawyer who handles many intellectual property matters, I understand the complexities that many small business owners, entrepreneurs, entertainers, authors, and other creatives face in this challenging area of the law. When you fail to protect your intellectual property, you relinquish your power and authority. Failing to protect your intellectual property is like opening the door to your home and letting a robber come into your home and take all your valuables.

You can schedule a short consultation with my office to discuss one of these issues or a comprehensive consultation to discuss several issues outlined herein. If you need help with business and brand clarity and expansion strategies, I recommend taking advantage of my business coaching options. Thriving **Beyond 2020** requires your proactive development of intellectual property protection strategies.

ABOUT THE AUTHOR
MICHELLE J. MILLER, ESQ., LLM

Michelle J. Miller, the Expansion Strategist™, is an international intellectual property, business & entertainment attorney. Michelle is also an international speaker, best-selling author, and business coach. She is the Founder & Chief Esquire Officer of The M. J. MILLER Law Firm®, the Creator of The Law Box®, and the Prophetpreneur Global University's Founder.™ In addition to her Bachelor's and Law degrees, Michelle has an advanced law degree (LLM) in International Business & Trade Law and a Doctorate of Ministry.

The M. J. MILLER Law Firm® is a boutique law firm focused on Trademarks & Copyrights, Business, Contracts, and Media/Entertainment. We provide confidential and excellent services to ensure that our clients make well-informed decisions to ensure clients receive maximum results from our business relationship. Michelle has over fifteen years of legal experience, primarily serving as a senior-level attorney in a corporate legal department before opening the firm. Michelle has extensive experience advising clients on cutting-edge legal issues on a local, national, and international level.

Michelle has created and negotiated multi-million-dollar contracts and provided primary legal support for business operations globally. Michelle's latest book, "REGISTERED: A Guide for Protecting Your Brand, Business and Bucks with Trademarks," is a #1 Amazon New Release and #9 Best Seller. Michelle's newest endeavor, the Prophetpreneur Global University™, is an online, faith-based business and prophetic marketplace ministry university that helps people excel in their industries while making money in ways that honor God. Overall, Michelle J. Miller – via The M. J. MILLER Law

Firm® -- is the undeniable law office of choice for business and brand protection and expansion.

TAPPING INTO THE SILVER LININGS OF DARK CLOUDS

ERIKA BLAIR MCGREW

The Covid-19 Global Pandemic has upended our lives in many ways; ways that we could never have imagined. But with every dark cloud, there is always a silver lining. Apart from the obvious, such as spending more time with family and deepening relationships, there are several money management and investing lessons that Covid-19 has taught us. Dr. Lynn and New W.E.A.LT.H. University have already schooled us on two foundational money management principles: 1) building up an emergency fund and 2) not relying on your 9-to-5 as your only source of income. I would like to add 3 Key Investment Principles for Thriving Amidst the Pandemic. The first is: **Get Started Now**: It is not about the money, it is about the mindset. The second is **Get Educated**: Take a foundational course on Investing so that you can make sound investment decisions. The third is to **Get an Accountability Partner** through a Financial Planner.

Get Started Now: It is Not About the Money, It is About the Mindset

There is an old saying that there is no better time than the present. That is extremely relevant amidst this pandemic. We have seen the stock market hit high's and low's during this time and it presents itself with a tremendous opportunity to get started investing. One of the main reasons that my course participants tell me why they do not invest is because they do not feel like they have enough money to get started. My response is always: It is not about the money... it is about the mindset.

Robert Kiyosaki writes in his books about the Cash Flow Quadrant (CFQ). The CFQ has been used by many individuals to guide their path to wealth. It takes an individual down a path from Employee (you have a job), to Self-Employed (you own a job), to Business Owner (you own a system and people work for you), to Investor (Money works for you.) The mindset is that we all want to get to the place of being an Investor where our money works for us, even while we sleep.

Another mindset shift is to think like billionaires think and move like billionaires move. A Forbes 2019 article entitled *How the World's Billionaires Got So Rich* lists the industries that afforded the billionaires their wealth. The No. 1 wealth producing industry was Finance & Investments, with 306 billionaires, or 14% of the billionaires list. Also, do you remember the 2011 movie *Limitless* that starred Bradley Cooper? If you recall, he took a pill that allowed him to fully utilize his brain. Where did the movie star go to gain wealth? You got it, he invested in the stock market!

The final mindset shift I will mention is that we have to start thinking like Owners and not just Consumers. Let me ask you a question… what are the things in your life that you cannot live without? Do you find yourself going by Starbucks every morning for coffee? Do you own Starbuck's stock? Do you buy every new iPhone when it comes out? Do you also have the Apple watch, Apple iPad or Mac computer? If so, do you own Apple stock? Are you constantly buying your kids Nike gym shoes? Do you own Nike stock? If you find that you are consuming the products and not being an owner, we need to do a small mindset shift. We can start small... by investing in just one share of the companies that we consume all the time. Did you know that at the time of this writing, one share of Apple stock can be bought for $119.05... this is cheaper than any Apple product on the market, even a refurbished one.

Get Educated: Take a Fundamental Course on Investing

Scripture says "Our people perish for the lack of knowledge." How many times have you heard this principle talked about? Well, it is true. Another big reason that my course participants tell me that they do not invest is because they do not feel like they have the necessary knowledge. This is through no fault of our own... the education system was built against us in this way.

Our traditional education system was built to teach us how to go and work for the wealthy and build their empires. You know the old age adage: go to school, get a good job with a good company, and work there for the rest of your life? How many schools, K-12 or Higher Ed, actually teach you how to obtain wealth? NONE!

You see, wealthy people talk about wealth principles at the dinner table or throughout everyday activities in their life. Whereas, non-wealthy people talk about "lack" or the "struggle" at the dinner table or throughout everyday activities in their life. Wealthy people seek out education and invest in themselves to get educated, which is the same thing you should be doing. One fundamental course that will get you well on your way to investing is the ***How to Invest in the Stock Market*** course (www.LearnWithLynnAndBlair.com). It is an innovative curriculum composed of two main parts: (1) Jumpstarting your Portfolio with ETFs and Mutual Funds and (2) Knowing your Investment BluePrint & Diversifying Your Portfolio. These are two foundational principles that will catapult your knowledge with investing and set your course for your investing journey.

Get an Accountability Partner through a Financial Planner.

The final Investment Principle for Thriving Amidst the Pandemic is to get an accountability partner. The sole reason for an accountability partner is to encourage you and to help you keep your commitments. How many times have you been excited about making a change in your life and you are steadfast and unmovable about seeing your change come to fruition? But then an obstacle in life comes along, the excitement fades, and you end up straying away from your decision? Usually, the first commitment that falls by the wayside is one dealing with your finances. Well, that is where a Financial Consultant, Financial Advisor, or Financial Planner comes into play.

The financial services industry has a long history of playing "semantics" with titles for financial professionals. Although there are no formal distinctions between the three titles, you can use the following definitions as a general guide. Financial consultants typically help people to solve an immediate financial problem, such as when they inherit money or receive a large financial settlement. Financial advisors typically help people understand their current financial situation and develop plans that help those people meet their short- and long-term financial goals. Many financial advisors are licensed to buy and sell financial products and have a focus on investments. Financial planners, on the other hand, are focused on assisting clients with building and protecting wealth by designing comprehensive, long-term financial strategies. Financial planners focus not only on investments but on specific goals such as Cash Flow Planning, Life Insurance Planning, Retirement Planning, College Planning, etc.

No matter the title, the most important trait for your accountability partner is that they operate under the Fiduciary standard and not just the Suitability standard. The ***Build Your W.E.A.L.T.H. Portfolio Bootcamp*** allows you to work one-on-one with me as your accountability partner. We'll develop strategies to ensure that you have a sufficient emergency fund, we'll evaluate your current retirement plans or investments to ensure that that they match your risk profile, and we'll set your lifestyle goals and develop investment strategies to meet them. You'll also get access to valuable education and training to implement the strategies that are developed.

Although the Covid-19 pandemic threw a serious curve ball for many of our plans in 2020, it also presented a unique opportunity to settle down and give serious thought to some areas of our lives that needed more attention. By *Getting Started Now*, *Getting Educated*, and *Getting an Accountability Partner,* you could be well on your way to Investing and building a legacy of wealth for your family for generations to come.

ABOUT THE AUTHOR
ERIKA BLAIR MCGREW

Erika "Blair" Mcgrew is a Wife, Mother, Finance Professor, and Financial Consultant. She believes that her power, passion, and purpose lies with helping to decrease the Wealth Gap for vulnerable communities. She does this by educating, empowering, and equipping individuals with the mindset, skills, and strategies used to build wealth.

She first sought to bridge the wealth gap by developing an education and empowerment program for high school students that teaches financial literacy and investing. She is the Founder and Principal Curriculum Designer for Young WallStreet Inc., a 501 c(3) non-profit. Since 2015, Young Wallstreet has taught high school students in Atlanta and Memphis how to build wealth through investing.

Erika currently works as a Financial Consultant with Advocacy Wealth Management and as an Adjunct Professor at Clark Atlanta University. She spends most of her time advising affluent clients and developing innovative investing curriculum for non-traditional clients.

Erika "Blair" is committed to social entrepreneurship and giving back. She has been awarded the President's Lifetime Achievement Award for Volunteer Service from the White House under President Barack Obama. She serves on the Advisory Board of Warrick Dunn Charities and holds leadership positions with National Coalition of 100 Black Women – MECCA chapter; National Association of Securities Professionals; CFA Society of Atlanta and Marietta Roswell Alumnae Chapter of Delta Sigma Theta Sorority, Inc. Erika "Blair's" background includes a B.S. in Electrical Engineering and an MBA in Finance. She is currently a Doctoral student in

Finance at the University of Memphis. She has been married for nineteen years to Christopher McGrew and has two sons, Londyn and Jonathan.

IT'S NOT EITHER OR; IT'S BOTH!

INGRID LAVON WOOLFOLK

Three Critical Steps to Balancing Employee & Entrepreneur

In 2009, I became the youngest Corporate Controller at a Fortune 100 company. This seemed like a dream that had been deferred for over 50 years, since my grandfather had migrated from the south, Haynesville Louisiana to be exact, in the mid 1930's with only 10 dollars and a desire for a life beyond picking cotton or working in the fields as his mother and father had done. I was grateful to have been able to see where my grandfather grew up, and I knew my great-grandfather as a hard working but ornery man. (He was just plain mean to most people). But here I was, accepting a job that no one in my family had ever done before. In actuality, I was a black girl working at one of the highest levels in finance with a single mother that consistently told me I was better than our current life and required me to act in that way.

This was also a culmination of life experiences. At the young age of 6, I counted the chicken dinners Big Mama sold to the post office down the street, and watched the races to track what numbers would come in after I had given the bets to the community bookie. Yes, I was the youngest bookie you'd ever meet, and a tough one at that. I didn't play a ton of sports, nor did I have a ton of hobbies, but what I did have was the ability to think in numbers and not words. I was also fortunate enough to live with a woman that worked a fulltime job and always had some type of side job whether it was at TJ Maxx or customer service from 5-9pm a few days a week.

Now I know; my mother, Geneva, was the first Corprenuer in my life. She worked her corporate job as a receptionist ultimately working her way up to paralegal assistant. But she also loved interior design and decorating, so she also did this on the side. Many ask, "how do you have the capacity to work a full-time job and still run a multiple 6 figure consulting company?", and my answer is always… that's all I know how to do! God built me this way. It's never been an either or for me; it's always been BOTH!

Beyond 2020 is going to require many of us to do both. There won't be any other options to take care our families, to reap what we lost from a global pandemic while continuing to try and create that "new normal" everyone references on a daily basis. We will shift into a season that will require us to dig deeper than ever before. But how do you do it? How do you dig deep in a place when you probably feel like you are at your lowest? Well, the good news is when you are at your lowest, that is the time where opportunity and preparation will collide and create the expansion your heart desires.

There are tons of examples of people working several jobs not to get ahead or to save for a vacation, but to buy groceries, pay rent, or keep the car from being repossessed. And I'm one of them. While my initial company was started out of a desire to help minority career women connect to opportunities they wouldn't have otherwise been able to gain access to in 2010, my 2015 side hustle quickly turned into the very thing that allowed me to survive during a divorce. And now, 5 years later that same business has turned into a company helping thousands of entrepreneurs and small businesses create financial statements, make more money than they ever have seen, and access over $50MM in government funding, grants, and resources. Imagine you taking the skills that you use every day and creating a vital company that changes lives. The goal is to do it before it does you!

As the saying goes, success leaves clues. So, I'm going to share with you my top 3 critical areas that enabled me to stay and thrive on both sides of the aisle for almost 10 years.

Change Your Mind!

Oprah said, "the key to realizing a dream is to not focus on the success but the significance, and then even the small steps and little victories along your path will take on great meaning." You must make up your mind to take the small step. If you're looking for money, you already have it. It's all in your mind. Many of us focus on the wrong things - the insignificant things. We concentrate so much on the success of others that we miss the opportunity to fuel the success in ourselves. We love to watch and celebrate others through social media while deep down not never believing we can also have what we see.

Start with a vision board or vision journal. Yes, they do work! Write what you want to see in your life. Spell it out. Be very specific about the color, the size, the amount, and the time. We pray for things, but because we are not specific enough, we accept the wrong thing thinking it was the right answer. Think of it this way, you get exactly what you ask for. Therefore, if you think big, ask big, and invest big, you will reap big.

Use What You Have

You already have a skill that can be monetized, you just haven't considered it in that way. We all have something that someone else needs or wants. Whatever you do in your 9-5, it can be offered in your own business. Bookkeepers can keep books for other businesses, attorneys can build their own practice offering counsel to a different segment of people, and even customer service representatives can provide virtual assistance to small businesses looking for part time support. Whatever you do, from being a trucker to working a cash register, it can be monetized for your own personal gain. Use this time! If you don't seize the moment to build a business while you're working for one, you would have missed the opportunity of a lifetime.

Nelson Mandela reminds us that, "it all looks impossible until it's done." Start one hour a day to focus on one action a week. Create one goal a month. Put an action plan together and set aside one hour a day to drive that goal. Every minute you execute gets you closer to accomplishing that goal. If you have a fulltime job, kids, husband, etc., use your lunch time at work or when the house is asleep to get that one hour accomplished. Don't worry about sleep; once you start this company, you'll make money while you're sleeping. Just get some rest, set aside the time, and get it done.

Set a Money Goal!
We all need additional income! Wealthy, rich, hood rich, or poor; we are all looking for an opportunity to make some more money. You don't make what you don't measure. All goals have to be quantified, especially those that have monetary opportunities attached to them.

Take inventory of your personal finances. Who do you OWE? Where are you lacking? Are you able to save? Are you able to give? Do you have everything you need? If you answered yes to all of those questions, then assess, what do you OWN? Use your new business income opportunity to purchase property, stocks, and invest in other businesses. At the end of the day, the goal in life is freedom. Freedom to work if you want, and not work if you don't. Freedom to give and not worry about paying bills, and the freedom to simply live the way God intended for us. Leaving a legacy to the world is the best form of freedom. I want my name etched in the side of a building for my grandkids kids to know that all of my work was for them. This additional income ability you have inside of you could be the next global solution. Never discount small beginnings, as most billionaires started in their basement with a dream and a desire.

Being an employee and an entrepreneur is tough. It is not for the faint at heart. There will be tears, there will be pain, there will be frustrations of comparison to others, and most importantly, there will be failures. The key is to fail fast and forward. Never allow the failure to stop you from moving on. 2020 has taught us that nothing and no one is absolute or absolved from the unknown. All plans can be foiled, but lack of planning can be fatal. Beyond 2020 is your opportunity to go out and create your wildest dreams, live your wildest life, and leave a legacy of wildness. That's it; that's my motto for Beyond 2020 - Live my wildest life. And you can do it to!

ABOUT THE AUTHOR
INGRID LAVON WOOLFOLK

Ingrid LaVon is a former corporate finance executive turned entrepreneur. She runs a boutique firm offering CFO and strategic management services to mid-sized companies. She also serves as a celebrity CFO to many entertainers. Like most divorcees, Ingrid LaVon threw herself into starting a new business and co-parenting her then four-year-old son while going through her second divorce. The journey to healing was hard, hurtful, and often disheartening. Her debut book, *Living After Divorce: 21 Ways to Heal and Move Forward*, is a testament to the fact that life doesn't end with divorce. Ingrid LaVon currently resides in the suburbs of Chicago with her new husband Lynn, and son Tate.

PRAY, PIVOT AND FIND YOUR PURPOSE IN A PANDEMIC

DEADRA WOODS STOKES, JD

January 1, 2020 was a New Year. I started the New Year attending The W.E.A.L.T.H. Experience, and annual empowerment event in Los Angeles, CA, at the urging of my longtime friend and confidant, Lynn Richardson. It was at this event that I wrote goals for 2020, completed a vision board, shed tears about plans to refocus, and shared new plans with like-minded inspired individuals. Three days after arriving, participating in workshops, and socializing with other motivated individuals, I left Los Angeles feeling prepared, renewed and hopeful for 2020.

None of us had any idea what was coming our way. We had no idea that a deadly virus was waiting in the midst. Our government, unfortunately, ignored the impact of a new deadly virus that was emerging from overseas: a virus that changed and continues to change the course of the world and the way we live. Who knew that something that is unseen to the naked eye, could have such great impact on the entire world? It is unfathomable to somehow grasp the potential impact of something we are unable to see with the naked eye, especially when conflicting information is being disseminated to society.

Society was receiving juxtaposed information from medical professionals warning about the deadly impact of a virus while the United States Commander in Chief simultaneously ignored those same warnings and communicated to all that it was nothing more than a "hoax" that would mysteriously "disappear" as quickly as it came. No one knew in January 2020 that life as we knew it was about to change. No one knew the individual decisions we would be forced to make to protect both our businesses and our families. No one knew that the entire world would be forced to make a paradigm shift in order to survive. Most importantly, no one knew that the United States was headed for events that would create the greatest divide that we could ever imagine in our country. No one knew that on top of managing a deadly virus while isolated in our homes, that we would witness the deadly killing of an unarmed Black man in a 9-minute recording while under the bended knee of a police officer. In a 9-minute video, the "bended knee" that Colin Kaepernick took which originally symbolized solidarity and protest to increase awareness for equality for the treatment of African Americans was the very same knee that ultimately killed an unnamed Black man. No one knew!!!!

However, COVID-19 is much like *Faith*! Hebrews 11:1 says, "Faith is the substance of things hoped for, the evidence of things not seen." As a Christian, I have over 50 years of experience knowing the impact of something unseen. As a believer in *Faith*, I knew how to appreciate the impact of something unseen, but made the paradigm shift to continue to thrive. So, trusting trained Medical Professionals, appreciating the warnings of COVID-19, and having *Faith*, I knew that managing the world as I knew it would require me to shift.

How do you shift when you are forced to stay home, isolate, take precautions, and protect your family?

It was during my required immobilization that I had to make the choice in the words of Andy Defrain from my favorite movie, *The Shawshank Redemption*, "You get busy living or you get busy dying!" Once I realized that the need to travel to appear in court proceedings, attend various legal matters, travel for meetings, etc. no longer existed, I realized I was given the gift of time. It was like angels had heard my pleas as I sped up and down highways running from one appointment to the next. So now with the gift of time, the choice became how should I use this time?

So, stuck at home in a Pandemic, what do you do? It comes down to three things! One, you PRAY! Two, you PIVOT! And Three, you rediscover your PURPOSE!

PRAYING IN A PANDEMIC
All around us, the number of infected people steadily increased and the deaths steadily climbed. This virus was not just serious, but it was deadly!!! Schools, restaurants, and court buildings were closed. The list of symptoms for COVID-19 were like those of the common cold, however, those persons who began experiencing respiratory issues suffered the worst, and oftentimes, passed away. Never in my lifetime was I informed to STOP!

Stay put!

Remain at Home!

You may say that you always pray, but this was the first time any of us had to pray during a Pandemic. Being immobilized in my home with my family, my prayer was different. First, my prayer was focused on safety, health, and protection for my family from COVID-19. However, my prayer then shifted to direction and guidance, and most importantly, what to do with the newfound time. How to use the time in the best way possible to achieve the best results. Most importantly, how would God want me to navigate at this time? What was the best way for me to navigate? Prayer would not only provide PEACE and PROTECTION, but PRAYER provided POSSIBILITIES!!!

Not certain about the next move, I simply began to move and tackle those things that I had ignored or simply did not have time to complete. I created a list of things that needed attention. As I tackled my life's "Things to Do" list, other opportunities and possibilities began to appear. As I took one step, doors began to open. Sometimes it is just that simple. Make a list of things you need to complete. Prioritize those things on your list. Break down the things on your list with simple manageable steps that cam be checked off one by one. As I began to tackle that list, opportunities began to appear.

What I realized is that the new "time" gave me the ability to conquer things that needed attention: the things my hectic schedule caused me to continuously ignore. Through prayer, I heard a small voice say, "make a list" and "check it twice!" Yup, just like Christmas. Tackling that list freed me from the burden of being overwhelmed and provided me with a spirit of accomplishment. As I accomplished and tackled things on my list, I felt energized to approach the next task. We were in a pandemic, but I was accomplishing items that had long been ignored. I realized that oftentimes, we make things more complicated than they need to be! So, whenever you find yourself at a new place, stop, pray, take a breath, make a list, and start checking off.

PIVOTING IN A PANDEMIC
As I conquered the list of those things that had been ignored, I realized that while I was in the same physical space, I simply made a slight turn and starting using my energy in another

space. This took me back to my childhood when I was enrolled in dance classes and learned an early dance move referred to as a "pivot." When a dancer is taught to pivot, she is instructed to rotate her body on its vertical axis without traveling in any direction. So, if you are dancing in one direction and have the need to turn to go in an entirely different direction, you are taught to stand still and turn while in the same place to reposition yourself to move in the next direction. You may find yourself turning and going back in the same direction, but when you do so, you will go back differently than when you came.

So, after you pray…YOU MUST PIVOT!!! Stand still and firm, write your list of things you need to do and those that you have ignored, overlooked or things that you have been too preoccupied to tackle, and then you PIVOT! You PIVOT and attack each item on that list! A certain sense of accomplishment begins to take over as you eliminate items on your list and de-clutter your life. Your thoughts become clear and you realize different opportunities that you were unable to see when you were juggling life.

Prior to COVID impacting our lives, we did not PIVOT as much as COVID required of us. Why? Because we simply moved forward during the course of the day in our regular routine. We would PIVOT when we were forced to do so, but soon thereafter, we would fall back into our regular routine. However, COVID required us to figure out how to remain in one place and PIVOT in one manner to complete a task and PIVOT shortly thereafter to conquer the next task. We found ourselves forever on that vertical axis rotating without traveling in any direction, yet moving (pivoting) to tackle the next thing on our list. It was and still is a Pandemic, but in all actuality, it provided us with an opportunity for "true" self-reflection.

We discovered how to talk to one another virtually in real time, conduct meetings, purchase and sell real estate and provide sound advice, all while remaining in one place. When we eliminated travel time, we saved money because we did not pass by our neighborhood coffee shop and purchase that $6.00 cup of coffee. No longer were we planning our next lunch date. Despite the world experiencing a Pandemic, we became exposed to a whole new world and we were all forced to make a paradigm shift. But as we made shifts, we realized that efficiency could still be achieved! However, the absolute best realization was that while we were required to PIVOT, our possibilities for success were unlimited.

FINDING YOUR PURPOSE IN A PANDEMIC

So first you PRAY, then you PIVOT, and naturally, you then discover your PURPOSE! In *The Purpose Driven Life* by Rick Warren, he tells us that we are NOT accidents. We are all here for a purpose and thus we all have the potential to achieve greatness. Greatness, however, is not measured by your monetary wealth or your worldly possessions, but it is identifying your purpose and fulfilling it to your absolute best. Warren goes on to describe how finding your purpose operates to simplify your life. It allows you to easily evaluate activities and determine whether it is consistent with your purpose or not. Realizing your purpose allows us to focus, and that ultimately leads to renewed energy and motivation. Prior to COVID, many of us were stressed, fatigued, and in conflict because honestly, what we really needed was a moment. Well, COVID made us do just that; it provided us with a moment to PRAY, an opportunity to PIVOT, and ultimately, to discover our PURPOSE.

ABOUT THE AUTHOR
DEADRA WOODS STOKES

As a licensed practicing attorney for over 22 years, Deadra Woods Stokes has developed a reputation as a leader and wealth advisor. She has earned the name the **Wealth Counselor** because of her sound legal advice to clients in the areas of Estate Planning, Probate, Real Estate, Bankruptcy Reorganization, and Business Succession Planning. Her insightful understanding of each client's personal needs and her hands-on approach has enabled her to serve as a legal advisor for over 1500 clients and their families.

Her outstanding leadership skills and exceptional business acumen were recognized through her selection as one of thirty-seven business owners out of approximately 200 applicants to participate in the first cohort group of the Goldman Sachs 10,000 Small Business Program in 2012.

In the legal community, Deadra is recognized as a woman of high personal integrity and one who is distinguished by exceptional client confidence and trust. In recognition of this, she and her legal team experience an 85% client retention rate and secure 99% of their business through client referrals.

Realizing her commitment to educating others in the law, she also serves as an Adjunct Professor at Governor's State University in University Park, Illinois. Her commitment and dedication to the community is further evidenced through her service as a board member and/or Officer for various not-for-profit organizations including, but not limited to, Delta Sigma Theta Sorority, Incorporated, United Way Southwest, RESPOND Now, JASSAC Foundation, South Suburban

Chicago Chapter of Jack and Jill of America, Incorporated and South Suburban PADS.

In her spare time, Attorney Stokes loves to read, exercise, and spend time with her husband of 16 years, their three daughters, her mother, and immediate family members.

CONCLUSION: THE BEYOND 2020 OATH

LYNN RICHARDSON®

Wow! After taking in all of this wisdom, journaling, praying and seeing my brand new existence Beyond 2020, I don't know what to say.

But there are a ton of things I'm ready to do! **Are you ready?**

If so, join me in taking this Beyond 2020 Oath:

I will follow Michelle Senderson's advice and remain ready for the changes ahead: both seen and unseen.

I take firm heed to Angelina Crosby-Pigott's guidance in the preparedness that comes along with a survival strategy and a get-away plan.

I will thrive as an entrepreneur and remember the example of Othelia Schultz in knowing what must be done when no one else is giving you a job.

I will mimic Nikki Cheree's strategy in using my five senses – sight, touch, taste, hear and smell – as I get back up again and move Beyond 2020.

I will open my eyes as advised by Dianne Bowdary, I will take inventory of my thoughts, actions, and money habits that deplete me and I will denounce those things in favor of peace and wealth.

I will be uapologetic in my efforts to create a new life for myself and I will establish new non-negotiables as Andrea Hayden advises.

I will establish new norms along with Dr. Vanessa de Danzine as I guide others along the path to financial freedom.

I will see the parallels of the pandemic and a viral financial existence as outlined by Virgie M. Bullie and I will use my M.A.S.K.S. always.

I will transform my thinking as Dr Catrina Pullum advises by accepting the losses, assessing the present, and ascertaining the future tomorrow and Beyond 2020.

I will learn the pandemic lessons that have impacted me, I will remain coachable, and I will retain the services of business coaches who provide wise legal counsel as so eloquently detailed by Syrena Williams.

I will protect my brand and treat my intellectual property like the gift that it is by implementing comprehensive trademark and copyright strategies outlined by Michelle J. Miller.

I will tap into the silver linings of life by establishing a financial strategy, and as Erika Blair McGrew shares, I will build my wealth portfolio with the support of an accountability partner.

I will not choose one part of me; rather I will embrace all of my gifts and follow Ingrid LaVon's lead as I change my mind, use what I have, and set money goals now and Beyond 2020.

I will pray, pivot and continue to seek my purpose in a pandemic, as shared by Deadra Woods Stokes, and I will do so no matter the circumstances as I thrive Beyond 2020.

ABOUT THE AUTHOR
LYNN RICHARDSON®

Named by Urban Influence Magazine as one of the 20 Hottest Influencers in America, Lynn Richardson® is an author, entertainment executive and celebrity financial coach who uses her quick wit and humorous presentation style to help others face their money issues and achieve personal, professional and spiritual harmony.   With more than two decades of leading roles in the banking and real estate sales industries, Lynn's vision is best portrayed in her books, most notably Living Check to Monday: The Real Deal About Money, Credit and Financial Security, which achieved Best Seller status at the Congressional Black Caucus Conference Book Pavilion.   Lynn is featured regularly on Good Morning America, Fox Business, Access Live, The Steve TV Show, The Hallmark Channel's Home & Family Show, BET Networks and has appeared in Essence, Jet, Upscale, on Get Up Mornings with Erica Campbell, The Tom Joyner Morning Show, and in countless media outlets nationwide. She has served as Chief of Operations for Russell Simmons' & Dr. Benjamin Chavis' Hip Hop Summit Action Network and is currently the President and CEO of MC Lyte's Hip Hop Sisters Foundation, and President and COO of MC Lyte's Sunni Gyrl entertainment and celebrity management firm -- where she oversees empowerment programs that impact the globe.   Lynn is also the President of **3 L Productions Inc**, a production firm in Hollywood responsible for new and upcoming tv/film projects.

Lynn is committed to nurturing her ministry for the benefit of others. She is the Pastor of Stewardship at California Worship Center under the leadership of Sr. Pastor Warryn Campbell and First Lady Erica Campbell. She and her best friend Demietrius have been married for over 26 years, they have three daughters, and they call a Los Angeles suburb home.